Singing the Story:

SIGHTINGS IN CHRISTIAN MUSIC

By Glen V. Wiberg

Glen V. Wiberg
I Cor. 4:1

Pietisten.

Seattle and Minneapolis

Singing the Story: Sightings in Christian Music

Pietisten, Inc., 7311 23rd Ave NE, Seattle, WA 98115

ISBN-13: 978-0-615-49535-4

ISBN-10: 0-615-49535-4

To the memory of Rev. *J. Irving Erickson 1914-1992*
for his passion in preserving the music of our forebears
and the hymnody of the historic church.

Contents

Foreword 1
Introduction 2
In the Lord's Courts 4
Hymn: What Joy There Is 6
Companions of All 8
Hymn: With God as Our Friend 12
A Friend Now and Forever 14
Hymn: Wheresoe'er I Roam 16
Zion's Happy Pilgrims 18
Hymn: Chosen Seed and Zion's Children 20
Grace for Today 22
Hymn: Day by Day and with Each Passing Moment 24
A Tender, Loving Moment 26
Hymn: Thy Holy Wings, Dear Savior 28
A Shout of Gladness. Alleluia! 30
Hymn: Lord of all Gladness 32
Revisiting our Early Origins 34
Hymn: Come, You Faithful, Raise the Strain 35
Hymn: The Day of Resurrection! 38
Sing It Again 40
Hymn: O Let Your Soul Now Be Filled with Gladness 42
The Feast is Waiting 44
Hymn: How Great the Joy 46
A Magic Moment 48
Hymn: Children of the Heavenly Father 50
God the Nurturer 51
Hymn: More Secure Is No One Ever 55
Hymn: Tryggare Kan Ingen Vara 56
Architect of Creation 58
Hymn: How Great Thou Art 60
Hymn: Our Mighty God Works Mighty Wonders 62
Surveying the Wonder 63
A Costly Sacrifice 69
Hymn: If Asked Whereon I Rest My Claim 71
Hymn: And Can It Be That I Should Gain 72

A Nobler Theme 74
Hymn: Sing my Tongue, the Glorious Battle 76
Hymn: At the Lamb's High Feast 77
With Many Voices 78
Hymn: Jesus of Nazareth Passes By 80
Hymn: I Sing With Joy and Gladness 81
A Singer of Passion 82
Hymn: He the Pearly Gates Will Open 84
Mercies Beyond Counting 85
Hymn: The Numberless Gifts of God's Mercies 87
Gathering at the River 88
Hymn: Shall We Gather at the River 90
Hymn: O How Blest to Be a Pilgrim 91
The Song of Life 92
Hymn: Let All the World in Ev'ry Corner Sing 94
Hymn: Rejoice in God's Saints 95
The Song Goes On 96
Hymn: Unexpected and Mysterious 99
Surrounded by Angels 100
Hymn: By Gracious Powers 102
Hymn: Surrounded by God's Silent, Faithful Angels 104
Practice in Christianity 106
Hymn: Behold a Host, Arrayed in White 108
The Legacy Lives On 110
Hymn: O Zion, Acclaim Your Redeemer 112
Hymn: Prepare the Way, O Zion 114
Thinking Globally, Singing Locally 116
Hymn: Seguirte Solo a Tí (We Worship Only You) 118
Communicating the Story 120
Hymn: Come Celebrate the Presence of the Lord 122
Welcome Sinners 124
Hymn: Amazing Grace! How Sweet the Sound 126
Epilogue: A Rich Legacy 127
Hymn: Fill the Earth with Music 130
Hymn: Let the Whole Creation Cry 132
Appendix: Recommended Recordings 133
Copyright Owners 135
About the Author 137
Acknowledgements 138
Index 139

Foreword

Music is in our hearts. Our musical heritage can be likened to the air we breathe; it often lies beneath conscious awareness. Treasured songs come into our minds and out of our mouths unbidden. With a full heart, Glen Wiberg brings us this thoughtful history in which vision and understanding come together in harmony.

The publishers and editors of the devotional journal *Pietisten* demonstrate fresh vision and love for this heritage by making available this collection of Pastor Wiberg's "Sightings in Christian Music," displaying with them the songs about which he writes. Glen Wiberg's columns have been a regular feature of the journal for years, following the death of J. Irving Erickson, who had written a similar column, "How We Got Our Hymns." Erickson is the author of *Sing it Again*, another volume very worth having.

Pastor Wiberg served on three hymnal commissions (for the 1973 and 1996 hymnals, as well as the 1990 *The Song Goes On* supplement) for the Evangelical Covenant Church—a mark of respect for his vision, his sense of music, poetry, and musical history. These pages reveal his love for and knowledge of Christian music—grounded especially in the creative and warm-hearted songs of the Swedish Lutheran Pietists.

Through the years, many people in the Covenant Church have experienced the encouraging blessings of Pastor Glen Wiberg and his wife, Jane, as they have endorsed younger people and their efforts without hesitation. Faithful to the words of the first of *Pietisten's* "Premises," they "intend blessing." Glen was early in blessing *Pietisten*, including hearty participation, participation that continues!

Over the past 25 years, a host of contributors who, like Gideon's 300, kept their hands on their swords while taking refreshment, have made and continue to make *Pietisten* a living conversation. "Sightings in Christian Music" is one such accompaniment. David Hawkinson, Peter Sandstrom, Tommy Carlson, Sandy Johnson, Bruce Carlson, Elder Lindahl, Arthur Anderson, Irene Ecklund, Tom Tredway, Art Mampel, Arvid Adell, Eric and Jennifer Ecklund-Johnson, Nels Elde, Max Carlson, Bob Bach, and Penrod have been among these contributors.

Congratulations to Karl Nelson, Mark Safstrom, and the rest of the new staff of *Pietisten* for conceiving, executing, and publishing this book. May it meet with strong success! May there be many more to come!

Phil Johnson
Editor Emeritus of *Pietisten*

Introduction

To enter fully into the hymns accompanying the essays in this volume, we will begin with the historical setting of the music of our Swedish heritage hymns. The late Dr. Karl A. Olsson, in telling the story of the Evangelical Covenant Church, described the early Covenanters, known as "Mission Friends:"

> The unifying experience of the Mission Friends was salvation. They were one in the Crucified. They gave the freest expression to this in their singing. The name "läsare" [readers] by which Mission Friends were designated in Sweden emphasized the importance of a devotional reading of the Bible and related literature; it would have been equally correct to call these people "singers." For nothing seems to have brought them closer to a union with Christ than the singing of their hymns. And in the hymns the constantly recurring theme is the friendship of Jesus in the vicissitudes of life and the final "closing" with him when the mists have vanished. (Olsson, *By One Spirit,* p. 221-222.)

The sources of the songs and hymns they sang came from two main streams. *"The Swedish Psalmbook"* (*Den Svenska Psalmboken,* 1819) consisted of stately Lutheran chorales, rich in objective and poetic content, as well as more informal songs of the spiritual Awakening, more subjective and less poetic, set to the rhythms of folk melodies. Later, many of the American gospel hymns from Dwight L. Moody and Ira Sankey revivals were translated into Swedish and became especially popular in many immigrant communities.

Today, singing is still important among Covenanters, even as our hymns have moved toward a greater diversity, including hymns from the time of ancient Israel to the present. In our hymnal, there has been a broadening into a wider ecumenical hymnody to include the music of our growing ethnic communities; it has enlivened our congregational singing. You will notice that while most of the hymns in this volume are taken from *The Covenant Hymnal,* we have borrowed from other denominational hymnals as well, and they from us.

In large part through the legacy of our hymnodist, the late J. Irving Erickson, the Covenant Church has become the primary custodian of the heritage music among the North American denominations with Scandinavian background. As our church family grows, we may ask, "What are the gifts in our heritage music that make it worth preserving?" I would suggest that this music is evangelical, easily learned, and therefore singable. When new members in my congregation hear a song for the first time, they often ask: "Where did this song come from? It is so easy to sing and so joyful."

But it is the themes themselves that make these songs so moving inasmuch as they reflect a personal relationship to Jesus. Karl Olsson mentioned one of the recurring themes—the friendship of Jesus. There are also other related themes, such as the love of the Father who is tender and gracious ("warning and comforting as none else could"); joy in the new life in Christ ("O let your soul now be filled with gladness"); and the communal joy of believers "all sharing together in the feast of the Lord." This immigrant community also found great hope in the songs of pilgrimage. Having exchanged their homes in Sweden for new homes in a strange land, suffering the pain and uncertainty of uprooting, they sang with longing and hope for the heavenly home, "O how blest to be a pilgrim, guided by the Father's hand, free at last from ev'ry burden we shall enter Canaan's land."

There are also hymns for special occasions such as baptism, the blessing of a child, confirmations, weddings, and funerals. Lina Sandell's classic hymn "Children of the Heavenly Father" has been the favored hymn covering all occasions even today. Other hymns for the seasons of the Church Year enrich our celebrations.

These themes from the early hymns of our tradition are but a small sampling of themes and hymns from other traditions, which together flow through our history—at times like a sparkling brook and at other times like a rushing stream. Unlike some praise songs devoid of struggle, doubt, anxiety, fear and lament, the best hymns of Pietism, whatever their source, are narrative hymns telling the story of our journey of faith and as such are honest statements of the human condition. So the title of this modest offering—Singing the Story—is fitting since underlying our human stories is the Great Story.

As far as I can tell, there's only one thing we know. We know the Story. We have learned about the God who could have remained sovereign and remote, but chose rather to become human. He lived among us, teaching, healing the sick, raising the dead, and then in suffering love, dying on a cross and rising on the third day to redeem us and bring to birth in us—and our world—the New Creation. With such a story, as the old hymn asks, "How can we keep from singing?" We must sing! This book invites the reader to join the song.

In the Lord's Courts

The hymn "What Joy There Is" has been in every Covenant hymnal since the first official hymnal in Swedish, *Sions Basun* ("Trumpet of Zion" 1908). J. Irving Erickson in *Sing It Again* says it is perhaps Sweden's greatest hymn about worship. This became my favorite hymn from the new "brown" hymnal in the 1930s as I grew up in the First Covenant Church of Kansas City. I still believe it was the best hymn in that book. The hymn's title in the brown hymnal was "In the Lord's Courts." That's the place to which we come each Sunday morning. "Here in his presence glorious it is so good to be."

At the age of five I didn't grasp all the poetic images of the hymn, but over many years of singing them, these words have become my personal language of faith. At five, the words sounded friendly. Among its imagery was light, joy, sun, beautiful, lilies, refreshing dew, taste, love, life, strength, blessings, and His care.

Surrounded by a community that knew my name, loved me, and believed that one day I would become a preacher, I felt the friendly images such as "blooming like lilies" become names and faces. There was Grandma Westerdahl, in whose ample lap I would often fall asleep during the evening service. Or Gabriel Warren, a sturdy Norwegian, who always stood at the church door giving me the same welcoming words he gave the grownups. Or old Emil Soderstrom, the tailor, who always had Swedish peppermints, *polkagrisar,* in his pocket for children—though I confess that when I saw him take out his false teeth during the sermon, I had second thoughts about eating more *polkagrisar.*

While still in childhood, learning to read, I sang the lines of the hymn for myself. "How beautiful the union of souls redeemed and free who hold with God communion in faith and purity." Again the words brought two more beautiful faces to mind. I loved to sit toward the front of the sanctuary beside my Grandpa Wiberg, with his gold-rimmed glasses, the neatly trimmed beard, and the sweet smell of Lucky Tiger Hair Tonic in his sandy hair. As a Swedish immigrant, he silently formed each word of Pastor Larson's sermon on his lips as if "to taste God's love sincere." Often I saw a tear fall down his cheek, and I knew Grandpa was one of "the redeemed and free."

"Holding with God communion in faith and purity," I saw the beautiful face of Otto Swanson speaking Bible words in his lovely accent and gentle voice while serving my folks the bread and wine of Holy Communion. Looking up into his face,

I felt that God must look like that. Then, one day when I was nine years old, I heard my folks say that Otto Swanson was very sick. I went upstairs to my bedroom and prayed he would get well, but the next morning he died. I went upstairs again and this time I cried. Now Mr. Swanson was "holding with God communion."

Toward my teens, in singing the hymn two things happened. I heard the gentle wooing of the Spirit in the invitation of the hymn, "Come, see the Lord's salvation and taste his love sincere…watch with his people here." Pastor Larson often spoke to us during confirmation about the importance and urgency of answering God's invitation and casting one's lot by watching with his people here. To be a Christian, one must choose. "Outside, the world makes merry unhappy 'mid its toys, but in God's sanctuary the soul finds heavenly joys."

I began to understand that being "outside" could be unfriendly and threatening. But "inside," among these funny little people of the Spirit there is "a circle blest," a friendly, gentle people with names and faces, grandmas with ample laps and grandpas who loved and tasted the word, older folks with Swedish mints for kids, and people who reminded me of God. All of these folks "in God's sanctuary," on the corner of 42nd Street and Terrace, "the soul finds heavenly joys." The choice seemed easy, even if it seemed at later times often less than easy.

One day in my fourteenth year, I said "Yes" to my baptism and my name was added to these people, though sometimes with "faltering footsteps." I am nevertheless thankful I have never looked back—except with gratitude for all I have been given. "Others have labored," says Jesus, "and you have entered into their labor." "Who then can be unwilling to join their circle blest?"

What Joy There Is

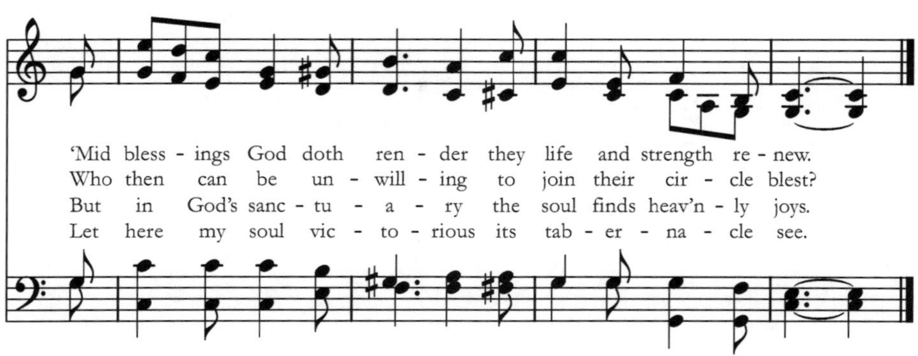

WORDS: Johan Ludvig Runeberg, 1804-1877, tr. A. Samuel Wallgren, 1885-1940
MUSIC: Johan Isidor Dannström, 1812-1897

7.6.7.6.D
Sanctuary

Companions of All

Through my friendship with Bernhard Erling, former professor at Gustavus Adolphus College in St. Peter, Minnesota, I was invited to be a presenter at "Gathering 2004" of the Augustana Heritage Association meeting in St. Peter. My subject was the common Swedish hymnody shared by the Augustana Lutheran Church and the Evangelical Covenant Church. Two years before, Philip Anderson of North Park Seminary had presented on our common history as Augustana Lutheran and the Covenant at the association's meeting in Lindsborg, Kansas.

The Augustana Church had been organized in 1860 as the Scandinavian Augustana Evangelical Lutheran Synod. It had a strong pietistic strain as it arose from the same movement in Sweden that gave rise to the Swedish Evangelical Mission Covenant Church of America, organized in 1885. In 1962, Augustana joined with four other Lutheran bodies to form the LCA—the Lutheran Church of America (now part of the ELCA). I was fortunate to be at the Augustana Church's final service (during which my brother-in-law was ordained!) held in Detroit, Michigan. I witnessed the merger there the next day.

The Augustana Historical Association meets every two years. More than 1,200 Lutherans from all over the country came to "Gathering 2004" in St. Peter to remember and to celebrate the history, liturgy, and music of Augustana as an empowerment for mission and service. The Augustana heritage is a gift to the larger Lutheran community to which its members belong.

The purpose of my session at Gustavus, using commentary and singing, was to explore the themes in our common Scandinavian hymnody in the conviction that they can be more than cherished icons of our immigrant past. The themes of the experience of Swedish immigrants are common to all immigrants and they are relevant as we learn how to host recent strangers from other countries in this new land.

I selected hymns with themes of *friendship* with Jesus, the crucified and living One. These hymns always include our longing to come closer to Jesus as our brother, friend, and Lord. There are also the themes of *fellowship* using metaphors taken from the family in which God is both mother and father, homey images that reflect intimacy and personal attachment to Christ. In the themes of *pilgrimage* in our music, one feels a certain wistful longing and loneliness for a better place, found in the songs of two homelands (Sweden and Heaven):

- "Thy Holy Wings, Dear Savior" by Lina Sandell;
- "Lord, As a Pilgrim," a Finnish hymn paraphrased by E. E. Ryden;
- "Wheresoe'er I Roam" by Carl Olof Rosenius, perhaps in response to the hymn;
- "Where is the Friend for Whom I'm Ever Yearning" by Johan Olof Wallin;
- "Jesus of Nazareth Passes By" by Anders Frostenson—a popular hymn in Sweden today that can be found in translation in the last two Covenant Hymnals (1973 and 1996), and
- "With God as Our Friend" by Carl Olof Rosenius.

I began my presentation with tributes to two hymnologists who have been very important in the preservation of our Scandinavian hymnody. The first, Augustana Pastor Ernest Edwin Ryden, is the author of *The Story of Christian Hymnody.* Ryden's book is the only definitive study in English I know of that deals with Scandinavian hymnody. Ryden also wrote several hymn texts in Covenant Hymnals. The other hymnologist I paid tribute to was the late J. Irving Erickson, author of *Twice Born Hymns* and the excellent handbook on *The Covenant Hymnal* (1963).

Through his service on two hymnal commissions, J. Irving was instrumental in the role the Covenant Church has had in preserving the music of Swedish heritage. Each hymnal has more than 30 English translations of Swedish hymns.

In re-visiting a few of the songs of our immigrant forebears, the question remains: What might our Lutheran/Covenant pietistic tradition mean today? This brings us back to the themes of *friendship, fellowship* in the family of God, and *pilgrimage.* They are more than cherished icons of our immigrant past, they are relevant in relating to the recent strangers in our land and relevant to 21st century humans who feel like aliens.

Martin Buber in *Tales of the Hasidim* records comments from Rabbi Barukh:

> He whom life drives into exile and who comes to a land alien to him, has nothing in common with the people there, and not a soul he can talk to. But if a second stranger appears, even though he may come from quite a different place, the two can confide in each other and live together henceforth, and cherish each other. Had they both not been strangers, they would never had known such close companionship. (*Tales of the Hasidim,* volume 1, p. 89.)

Today, in long stretches many of us feel as if we are living in a different land, a changing society and culture. As sojourners on the earth, bound for another city, we are the aliens, misplaced and lost because the familiar landmarks of home have been shifting and changing, some even removed. In short, we are becoming pilgrims like our immigrant mothers and fathers. We are the second strangers.

But this is also our great opportunity. Loosed from bondage to the comfortable, familiar, and domesticated, we as Christians can discover a new role as second strangers. We can become hosts to new immigrants who are strangers to the church. As bearer of the Gospel, the church is forever confronted with the new. In the words of the Rabbi, "had they both not been strangers," think of what both would have missed. We have a language in our hymnody of God's *friendship, family,* and *pilgrimage* that still speaks to the heart. There will be new music, too, that won't sound the same, the rhythm and beat will be different and jarring to some, but the story of pilgrimage and God's friendship "with brethren partaking the bread of our Lord" will be the same.

In the joyful gathering of 2004 at Gustavus with vigorous singing, lively liturgy, and preaching in the spirit of Augustana, both Jane and I felt like we were coming home.

"In re-visiting a few of the songs of our immigrant forebears, the question remains: What might our Lutheran/Covenant pietistic tradition mean today? This brings us back to the themes of *friendship, fellowship* in the family of God, and *pilgrimage*. They are more than cherished icons of our immigrant past, they are relevant in relating to the recent strangers in our land and relevant to 21st century humans who feel like aliens."

With God As Our Friend
1 With God as our Friend, with his Spir - it and Word,
2 In per - il - ous days, through the gloom of the night,
3 The Pil - lar that guides us through per - il and strife,
4 O Shep - herd, a - bide with us, care for us still,
all shar - ing to - geth - er the feast of the Lord,
a host march - es on through the dark - ness to light.
the Rock that is cleft, giv - ing wa - ters of life,
and feed us and lead us and teach us your will,
we face with as - sur - ance the dawn of each day
Not man - y, nor might - y, dis - owned by the world,
is Christ and his cross: by his Spir - it and Word
un - til in your heav - en - ly fold we shall sing
and fol - low the Shep - herd; and fol - low the Shep - herd,
they fol - low their lead - er; they fol - low their lead - er;
the heart he re - fresh - es, the heart he re - fresh - es,
our thanks and our prais - es; our thanks and our prais - es,

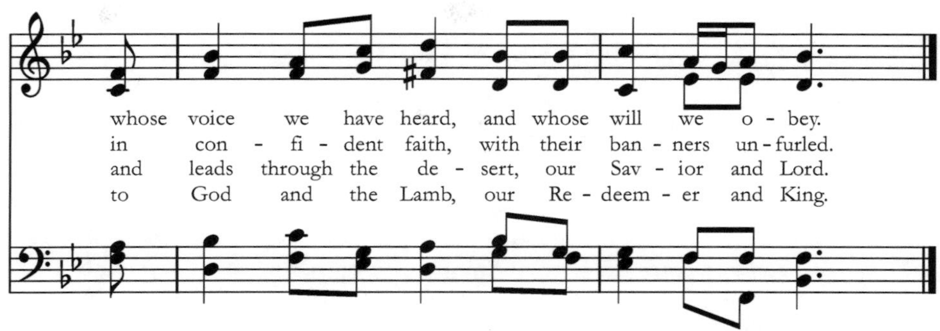

WORDS: Carl Olof Rosenius, 1816-1868, tr. © 1978 Lutheran Book of Worship 11.11.11.6.6.11
MUSIC: Oscar Ahnfelt, 1813-1882; arr. James P. Davies, 1913-, © 1973, 1996 Covenant Publications Ahnfelt

A Friend Now and Forever

Prior to our own hymnals and song-books was the hymnal of the Church of Sweden, *The Swedish Psalmbook*. This was the major literary achievement of Archbishop Johan Olof Wallin (1779-1839). Among the 500 hymns in the psalm book, Wallin wrote 128 original hymns, made 178 revisions, and translated 23 hymns from the German chorales. E.E. Ryden says in his fine book *The Story of Christian Hymnody,* "Some of the enduring quality of Wallin's hymns are reflected in the fact the Church of Sweden did not make a single change in his hymn book from 1819 for 101 years."

As Wallin was a poet and hymnodist in the high church's classical tradition, it's not surprising that Wallin had a profound dislike for the songs from the Pietistic tradition gathered in *The Songs of Moses and the Lamb* (first printed in 1717) and that he also disliked songs from the Moravian tradition, which had been in wide circulation in certain circles of Swedish piety. If he had lived to hear the songs of the revival movement from Rosenius, Ahnfelt, and Sandell, he would most likely have expressed a similar distaste.

This hymn by Wallin in *The Swedish Psalmbook* was well-known if not popular.

> Where is the Friend for whom I'm ever yearning?
> My longing grows when night to day is turning.
> And though I find Him not as day recedeth,
> My heart still pleadeth.

He searches in nature and beauty for intimations of this Friend, but then finally concludes that only in heaven will this yearning be filled:

> Soon on the shore where stormy wave ne'er breaketh
> The weary dove its final refuge taketh;
> The timorous lamb shall by the Shepherd's favor
> Find rest forever.

One of the best examples of a hymn from Oscar Ahnfelt's *Spiritual Songs* is "Wheresoe'er I Roam." Some months before his death, Karl Olsson said to me that this hymn by Carl Olof Rosenius expresses better than any other the theme of the revival movement hymn, namely, the believer's mystical, intimate fellowship with the crucified and risen Jesus as Friend. One wonders if it was written to answer Wallin's poignant question, "Where is the Friend for whom I'm ever yearning?" At any rate, the two hymns represent the contrast between the piety of the established state church and the revival movement: the objective psalmody of *The Swedish Psalmbook* and the subjectivity of the more folk-type music of Ahnfelt's songbook.

Wheresoe'er I roam, through valleys dreary,
Over mountains, or in pathless wood,
Ever with me is a Friend to cheer me,
Warning, comforting as none else could.
'Tis the Shepherd, who once dying, bleeding,
Now through all eternity shall live.
Jesus leads his flock, protecting feeding,
And the tend'rest care does give.

The message of the revival movement was plain. We don't need to wait until we reach the final shore in Heaven to have that yearning for friendship filled. The Crucified and Risen One can be known here and now as Friend walking ever beside us with wise counsel, comfort, and good cheer. And if Wallin's "timorous lamb" shall at last find rest and favor, Rosenius' vision of the final, gladsome meeting is anything but timorous:

To your presence–for this life is fleeting—
Take me, wash my garments in your blood;
And with Thomas may I, at your meeting,
Cry with joy, "My Lord and God!"

(Hymn 427, *The Covenant Hymnal: A Worshipbook*)

I am glad that Wallin asks the question, which is the human question, one we have all asked in our painful journey with less than certain faith, "Where is the Friend for whom I'm ever yearning?" But I am also glad that Rosenius says that Heaven does not need to wait for some final assurance of favor, but that the Friend is ever with us even when "I often feel forsaken, lonely." Perhaps this is why I count this hymn as one of my favorites.

Wheresoe'er I Roam

WORDS: Carl Olof Rosenius, 1816-1868, tr. Victor O. Peterson, 1864-1929, © Fortress Press 10.9.10.9.10.9.10.7
MUSIC: Ahnfelt's *Sånger*, 1868 Var Jag Går

Zion's Happy Pilgrims

I recently finished reading for the second time the English translation of *Lewi's Journey,* an engaging novel by Swedish author Per Olof Enquist. It brings together fiction and history and makes for fascinating reading. A friend of mine in Sweden, Dr. Inger Selander of Lund University, has lectured on the novel in Sweden and Germany. She states that "some of what the author does is close to actual occurrences, while other aspects of the factual may be questioned." It is the story of the two men, Lewi Pethrus and Sven Lidman, who were instrumental in bringing the Swedish Pentecostal movement from obscurity into the largest denomination outside of the national Church of Sweden in the 20th century.

What I found fascinating in the novel was the profound influence of the 18th century Moravian revival movement in northern Sweden on our own 19th century movement, extending even to the 20th century Pentecostal movement. The similarities are striking. Adherents of the Moravian revival were also called *"readers"* because of their use of the Bible and other spiritual literature. Other similarities of the 18th century revival include lay preaching, informal *"conventicles,"* the need for inner conversion, and a stress on the free grace of God through the blood of Christ.

Enquist makes frequent references in the novel to the influence of Moravian hymnody on the *Evangeliska Fosterlands-Stiftelsen* (The Evangelical Homeland Foundation), the revival wing of the Church of Sweden, which was Enquist's heritage. *Lewi's Journey* shows the influence of the music and theology of the Moravians on the Pentecostal movement and other free churches, including the Covenant, both in Sweden and in America. Our first official hymnal *Sions Basun* contained a section of fourteen hymns on "The Cleansing Blood of Jesus," which is the strong emphasis of Moravian hymnody. As Karl Olsson said, "the blood and wounds suggest primarily the suffering and atoning love of Christ in which the soul may rest."

In the early 1950s, Karl Olsson gave a lecture, "Covenant Beginnings: Mystical." He noted the preoccupation of the hymnody of the Swedish Moravians with bloody imagery, such as "swimming in Jesus' blood" and becoming "little blood worms who would live happily in his wounds." This is not entirely absent from our own early lyrics. Fortunately, such imagery has been refined and modified in the songs of the 19th century.

One of the more refined and modified hymns from the Swedish Moravians of the 18th century, "O Let Your Soul Now Be Filled with Gladness," is still one of the favorite hymns among Covenanters, who seem to have no trouble with the blood imagery in the phrase of verse 1.

> O let your soul now be filled with gladness,
> Your heart redeemed, rejoice indeed!
> Oh may the thought banish all your sadness
> That in his blood you have been freed..."

Another trace of a familiar Moravian theme comes in verse 3.

> Praise be to You, O spotless Lamb,
> Who through the desert my soul are leading
> To that fair city of joy exceeding,
> For which you bought me as I am.

Our Covenant hymnodist, J. Irving Erickson, saw this as a good example of the type of Moravian hymnody popular in the mid-1700s which speaks "of a spirit that is freer and more joyous than that of the average Pietist." The author of the text is Peter Jonsson Aschan (1726-1813), who was active in Moravian circles as principal of the school in Växjö in southern Sweden and who wrote poetry with a Moravian emphasis.

I have two observations from my reading of *Lewi's Journey*. First, in revisiting the Moravian tradition in Scandinavia, it is important to recognize that the Covenant Church didn't begin with the Rosenian movement of the mid-19th century as some may be inclined to believe. Its leader, Carl Olof Rosenius, lived from 1816-1868. Swedish Moravian "readers" were on the scene several generations earlier and contributed significantly to the movement from which we came. My other observation from *Lewi's Journey* is that, among the Swedish Moravians, there was a refusal to institutionalize their movement, which happened with other free churches. They just faded away, willing to be and do as Jesus said, "Unless a grain of wheat falls into the earth and dies, it remains just a single grain; but if it dies, it bears much fruit" (John 12:24). In a time when bigger is better, when church growth seems to be our highest priority, it is good that we remember the legacy of our Moravian forbearers.

My biggest surprise in the novel, however, was to discover that Lewi Pethrus' earlier leadership in the socialist cause continued to reflect his later strong social engagement as a Pentecostal leader in the cause of the poor. The institutionalizing of the Pentecostal movement served to divert him from his earlier passion, a regret he expressed on his deathbed.

Chosen Seed and Zion's Children

WORDS: Anders Carl Rutström, 1721-1772, tr. Claude W. Foss, 1855-1935, alt. — 8.7.8.7.D.
MUSIC: attributed to Anders Carl Rutström, 1721-1772; arr. *Sions Nya Sånger,* 1854 — Lammets Folk

"Lina Sandell wrote these words of poetry to give comfort and assurance as help against the pressures and anxieties of the day."

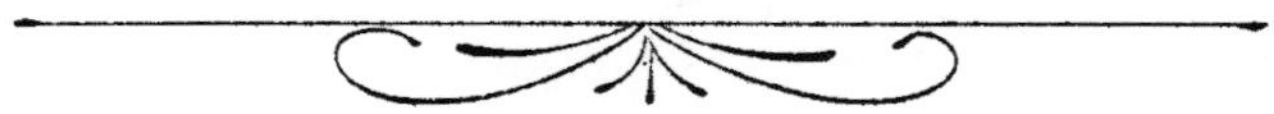

Grace for Today

Without doubt, the most popular hymn writer of the revival movement in 19th century Sweden was Carolina Wilhelmina Sandell-Berg, known more commonly as Lina Sandell (1833-1903). If a vote were taken today among Covenanters as to their favorite hymn, I would think that a close second to "Children of the Heavenly Father" would be her hymn, "Day by day and with each passing moment." As one of the favorites, this hymn has appeared in English translation beginning with *Mission Hymns* and the *Covenant Hymnals* of 1931, 1950, 1973, and 1996. For many who grew up with these hymns, those songs embrace the beginnings and endings, the baptisms and funerals of our Christian stories.

Lina Sandell wrote many songs about the heavenly Father's care, and one that immediately comes to mind is, "O Tender, Gracious Father." There were also a few hymns comparing God's care to a mother's, such as "Thy Holy Wings, Dear Savior"—a theme more common in Moravian hymnody. The father theme in Ernest Edwin Ryden's translation of "Day by Day" in the 1950 Covenant Hymnal, as well as the hymnals of the Augustana Lutheran Church, contained these lines, a literal translation from Swedish hymnals:

> Thou dost love more tenderly than ever
> Earthly father careth for his own.

However, Lina Sandell's original thought and language was this, "He who cares for me with a *mother's* heart."

What happened? We can only surmise that when it was published in Oscar Ahnfelt's collections of *Spiritual Songs* (*Andeliga Sånger,* 1850-1877), the editors changed the author's intention to "father's heart." The most popular translation of the hymn, by A.L. Skoog, retains the "father" metaphor by speaking of the "Father's wise bestowment." Sandell actually described God as mother on several occasions, a fact which the contemporary Swedish Christian vocalist Carola has brought to our attention in her popular 1998 recording of Sandell's hymn, *"Modersvingen"* ("The mother's wing") and other songs. But let's chalk one up for the feminists in the revival movement even though they lost the first round. And the moral? Better watch these translators, editors, and hymnal commissions!

But apart from language and translation, we need to remember that Lina Sandell wrote these words of poetry to give comfort and assurance as help against the pressures and anxieties of the day. When those words of "Day by Day" first appeared, they were accompanied with an allegory about an old wall clock that suddenly stopped. The dial decided to investigate and discovered that the pendulum was at fault. It had become bored and tired of swinging back and forth 86,400 times each day. "Try swinging six times," said the dial. The pendulum agreed and admitted that that would not be as wearisome. "But it's not six times, or sixty; it's the thought of six million times that disturbs me." "Bear this in mind, however," said the dial, "that while in a single moment you can think of the millions of swings you must make in a lifetime, only one at a time will be required of you. And no matter how often you must go through the same movements, you will be given a moment for each one." The pendulum admitted that it had acted foolishly in going on strike and promptly resumed its work.

Sandell then commented on the allegory, saying that it is foolish to put future burdens upon the present moment. We are given only a day at a time and for each day new grace, new strength, new help. She followed this by quoting Leviticus 33:25, "Thy shoes shall be iron and brass; and as thy days, so shall thy strength be." Then the text of the hymn followed with its practical wisdom, "Live today. Don't worry about tomorrow. Take a day at a time. Trust in the Lord."

Day by Day and with Each Passing Moment

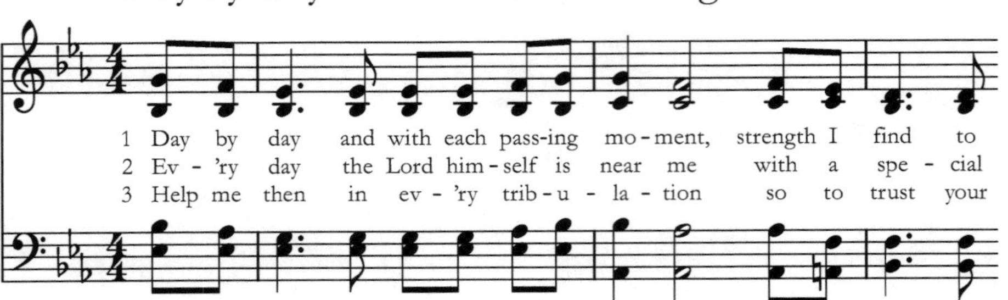
1 Day by day and with each pass-ing mo-ment, strength I find to
2 Ev-'ry day the Lord him-self is near me with a spe-cial
3 Help me then in ev-'ry trib-u-la-tion so to trust your

meet my tri-als here; trust-ing in my Fa-ther's wise be-stow-ment,
mer-cy for each hour; all my cares he fain would bear, and cheer me,
prom-is-es, O Lord, that I lose not faith's sweet con-so-la-tion

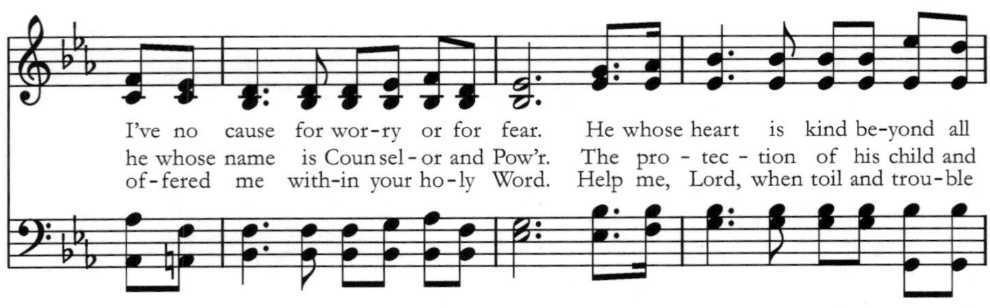
I've no cause for wor-ry or for fear. He whose heart is kind be-yond all
he whose name is Coun sel-or and Pow'r. The pro-tec-tion of his child and
of-fered me with-in your ho-ly Word. Help me, Lord, when toil and trou-ble

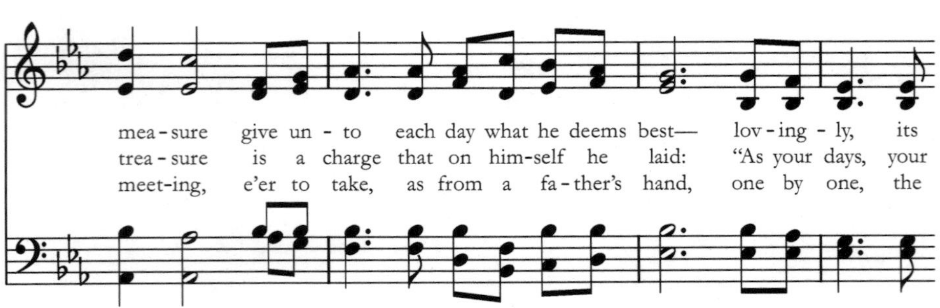
mea-sure give un-to each day what he deems best— lov-ing-ly, its
trea-sure is a charge that on him-self he laid: "As your days, your
meet-ing, e'er to take, as from a fa-ther's hand, one by one, the

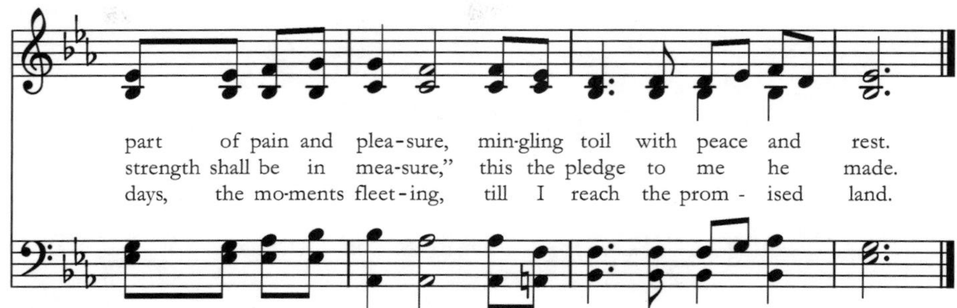

WORDS: Lina Sandell, 1832-1903, tr. A.L. Skoog, 1856-1934
MUSIC: Oscar Ahnfelt, 1813-1882

10.9.10.9.D.
Blott En Dag

A Tender, Loving Moment

(Co-written with Jane Wiberg.)

Many years ago, we attended the summer school at the University of Oslo, Norway sponsored by St. Olaf College. We were two kids right out of college, married only a few days, going to school together with two hundred American students in a strange land, enjoying it but also a bit homesick at times. However, on our first Sunday in Oslo, we attended the Bethlehem Mission Covenant Church, where we had the good fortune of meeting a lovely family, Helena and Olaf Ramstads. About eight weeks into our stay, they invited us for a weekend in their summer home high in the mountains of central Norway.

That Friday in August had been cold with a constant downpour. After our morning class, Olaf picked us up at the university and we began the long ride in rain and fog through the countryside. We thought we would never get there. We were tired and hungry, with no fast-food restaurants along the way. After many hours, the road became little more than a cow path until finally it disappeared. "Now," said Olaf, "we have to walk the rest of the way." Lugging our bags and supplies through brush and stumbling over stony ground we made our way up the steep incline. It seemed like a Norwegian mile.

Then we were there. The door of the mountain home was flung open with a hilarious welcome. After the hugs and kisses and the laughter of their five children with a mixture of Norwegian and English chatter, we entered a large room. It was ablaze with what seemed to be a hundred candles, a room of light wood with warm rosemaling colors in blue, red, and gold, a scene which only the romantic Swedish illustrator Carl Larsson could have adequately captured. With the table set and the delicious aroma of food filling the air, the feast began. Food never tasted better—ham, fresh rye bread, cheese, and lingonberries, followed by our favorite dessert—a caramel-crusted custard, then afterwards, good strong coffee in the living room.

Finishing our final cup, the fog suddenly lifted and sunlight brighter than candles filled the room. This was the signal for the white-haired patriarch to lead the family out onto the deck of the cottage. You can't imagine the breath-taking sight. With the fog lifted, we could see for the first time the majestic mountains of Hallingdal and the green valley below with emerald of yellow flowers, grazing cows and sheep with their little tinkling bells, as the sun cast long shadows of benediction over this pastoral scene.

Now came the time for the evening hymn. The old pastor with his fog-horn voice led the family in a song which we had never heard. "Bred dina vida vingar, O

Jesus över mig." Tears filled our eyes. We felt as close to heaven as one could. No longer homesick, we were home, surrounded by Christian friends, sheltered by the comfort and warmth of God's protecting grace. Imagine then our delight when in the following year, we were able to sing this hymn by Lina Sandell from our new Covenant Hymnal, 1950's "green" hymnal:

> Thy holy wings, dear Savior, spread gently over me;
> And through the long night watches I'll rest secure in thee.
> Whatever may betide me, be thou my hiding place,
> And let me live and labor each day, Lord, by thy grace.

We will never sing that song without picturing that scene looking out over the valley of Hemsedal surrounded by the mountains of Hallingdal, a tender, living memory from our honeymoon trip to Norway.

My history with this hymn continued with meeting its translator (whom I mentioned earlier), E. E. Ryden, in the late 1950s. I met him while serving in Princeton, Illinois where I was invited to speak to a group of Augustana Lutheran pastors at their monthly meeting. Knowing I was a Covenant pastor, the first question he asked was how our Covenant people had received and used this hymn he had translated, "Thy Holy Wings." I assured him it was one of the new and most loved hymns in our 1950 hymnal, where it first appeared. He then pulled a piece of paper out of his coat pocket and asked me if I would play a Finnish hymn he had just translated, "Lord as a Pilgrim." This hymn has appeared in our last two Covenant Hymnals due to that meeting.

Soon after coming to Minneapolis, I met Gracia Grindal (Professor of Rhetoric at Luther Seminary in St. Paul), a great Pietist friend who shared with me her version of "Thy Holy Wings," with a text revised for the baptism of her niece.

> Thy holy wings, O Savior, spread gently over me
> And let me rest securely through good and ill in thee.
> Oh, be my strength and portion, my rock and hiding place,
> And let my evr'y moment be lived within thy grace;
>
> Oh, let me nestle near thee, within thy downy breast
> Where I will find sweet comfort and peace within thy nest.
> Oh, close thy wings around me and keep me safely there.
> For I am but a newborn and need thy tender care.
>
> Oh, wash me in the waters of Noah's cleansing flood.
> Give me a willing spirit, a heart both clean and good.
> Oh, take into thy keeping thy children great and small
> And while we sweetly slumber, enfold us one and all.
> *(Worship [Ev. Lutheran], Hymn 613)*

Another tender, loving memory. And I have no doubt that Lina Sandell would approve and say, "Amen."

Thy Holy Wings, Dear Savior

WORDS: Lina Sandell, 1832-1903, tr. Ernest Edwin Ryden, 1886-1981, © Ernest Edwin Ryden
MUSIC: Swedish melody, arr. Mark S. Dickey, 1885-1961, © William K. Provine

7.6.7.6.D
Holy Wings

"What gives the hymn a special joy to me is that the song goes on, for with God life is a doxology in which we sing ourselves free of sadness, bondage, powers of darkness, sin, and death."

A Shout of Gladness. Alleluia!

In the higher churches, the "Alleluias" in the liturgy are eliminated during the penitential season of Lent, thereby holding them in reserve for the cascading "Alleluias" of Easter. However, there are occasions when the "Alleluia" cannot be repressed, often erupting in unlikely places where we least expect it.

In 1983, Carl Philip Anderson and I led a group of twenty people from our congregations on a trip to Israel. The schedule provided for a three-day layover in Switzerland as a time of rest and recovery before returning home. One of those days, a Sunday, we walked in the early morning through the abandoned streets of Zurich in search of Grossmünster, the church of Zwingli, the Swiss Protestant Reformer of the 16th century. Due to its massive towers against the skyline of the city, it was not difficult to find.

As we walked up the steps of the great cathedral, past the statue of the Reformer clutching a sword and the Bible, the great bells began to toll, a piercing sound whose memory still sends shivers up my spine. Upon mounting any church steps for worship, my pulse always beats faster in anticipation. But this was soon dissipated by the somber surroundings inside. A massive baptismal font stood before a stark, empty chancel without an altar or table or cross—appropriate, I suppose, to Zwingli's non-sacramental teaching.

The entire service was led from the high pulpit by the presiding minister. The seventy-five or so worshipers sat passively in the dim light of the cathedral. The sermon was delivered without hint of passion. But the final hymn brought a glimmer of recognition. Though it was sung in a dirge-like solemnity, the joy could not be altogether repressed. Four times during this Reformation hymn we sang Alleluia. The tune was engaging and the text strong. The person in our group sitting next to me said that this hymn was what made the service for her an act of worship and that it should be translated for Covenanters to sing. I agreed to make the effort.

In presenting this hymn by Johann Lindemann (1549-1631) to the committee of *The Song Goes On,* I was asked to take an older English translation by Catherine Winkworth (1829-1878) and rework it—which I did. It was accepted both in the supplemental hymnal and by the Hymnal Commission in *The Covenant Hymnal: A Worshipbook*. The hymn is "Lord of All Gladness." (In other traditions, the hymn is titled "In Thee is Gladness.")

My own sense of the music is that it should be sung with an accompaniment of ancient instruments including tambourines and castanets as if it were a Renaissance dance. I have a hunch that's what the tunesmith, Giovanni G. Gastoldi (1556-1622), originally had in mind. What gives the hymn a special joy to me is that the song goes on, for with God life is a doxology in which we sing ourselves free of sadness, bondage, powers of darkness, sin, and death. Even beyond sight, our timid voices blend in praise with the church triumphant in joy unending. Whether in Lent, in a bleak sanctuary, in the purgatory of doubt, or even at the grave, the "Alleluias" are our song!

Lord of All Gladness

WORDS: Johann Lindemann, 1549-1631, tr. Catherine Winkworth, 1829-1878, Glen V. Wiberg, 1925-, alt. Irregular
MUSIC: Giovanni G. Gastoldi, 1556-1622, © 1969 Concordia Publishing House In Dir Ist Freude

Revisiting our Early Origins

It was an unforgettable moment sitting in a Christian ethics class taught by Professor H. Richard Niebuhr at Yale Divinity School. At first I wondered if I had heard him correctly, but it was a seminal statement that would continually unfold in my subsequent years as a believer and a theologian. His statement was, *"To be a Christian you must first become a Jew."* Beyond the shock of the moment, it speaks truth every time I open the Sacred Book that combines the two testaments, or whenever I pray the Psalms or sing the *Gloria Patri* or the hymns of Easter.

Let's test Niebuhr's thesis by looking at three Easter hymns in *The Covenant Hymnal* and reflect together on the joining of the two traditions, the two stories and the two testaments.

> *Hymn 247 (verse 1) — Come, You Faithful, Raise the Strain*
> Come, you faithful raise the strain of triumphant gladness
> God has brought his *people* forth into joy from sadness.
> Now rejoice, Jerusalem, and with true affection
> Welcome in unwearied strains Jesus' resurrection.

The Lutheran hymnal, *Evangelical Lutheran Worship* (2006) makes the connections between the testaments even clearer:

> *Hymn 363 — Come, You Faithful, Raise the Strain*
> Come you faithful raise the strain of triumphant gladness!
> God has brought Is-ra-el into joy from sadness,
> Loosed from Pharaoh's bitter yoke Jacob's sons and daughters
> Led them with unmoistened foot through the Red Sea waters.

The good news is that the God who brought Israel out of Egypt also brought Jesus out of the tomb. There are two stories—Exodus and Easter—by the one and the same God who looked upon the suffering of his people, took notice and brought rescue.

> *Hymn 260 (verse 1) — The Day of Resurrection*
> The day of resurrection! Earth, tell it out abroad,
> The Passover of gladness, the Passover of God.
>
> From death to life eternal, from earth to heav'n on high,
> Our Christ has brought us over with hymns of victory.

The Passover refers to the *angel of death* passing over the homes of Israelites who had placed blood on their doors. It also speaks of the final meal eaten in haste before passing over the Red Sea "with unmoistened foot." We sing with Miriam's song of victory at the parting of the waters, even as "Christ has brought us over with hymns of victory." Passover and Easter by one and the same God.

Hymn 556 — At the Lamb's High Feast
At the Lamb's high feast we sing praise to our victorious King,
Who has washed us in the tide flowing from his pierced side, Alleluia!

Praise we him, who love divine give us sacred blood for wine,
Gives his body for the feast—Christ the victim, Christ the priest. Alleluia!

Where the paschal blood is poured death's dread angel sheathes the sword;
Israel's hosts triumphant go through the wave that drowns the foe. Alleluia!

Praise we Christ, whose blood was shed, paschal victim, paschal bread
With sincerity and love eat we manna from above. Alleluia!

The *Evangelical Lutheran Worship* hymnal has three additional verses (Hymn 362), with the last verse as a doxology:

Father, who the crown shall give,
Savior, by whose death we live,
Spirit, guide through all our days:
Three in One, your name we praise.
Alleluia!

The Covenant Hymnal has placed it in the section on communion hymns, but it is also an Easter hymn. The Passover and Exodus themes are woven into the Easter victory and the Holy Supper, where we receive and eat the manna from above. Passover and the Lamb's Feast, gifts of the one and the same God.

In the musical gifts of the Easter season, I would commend to you one of Johan Sebastian Bach's earliest cantatas, based on Luther's hymn *"Christ Jesus Lay in Death's Strong Bonds,"* Cantata 4. As in the hymns above, its text contains similar themes, the *Christus Victor* motif. In Christ, God has won the victory and those who know it are compelled to sing. With multiple voices each verse is sung.

There was a wondrous war between Life and Death.
Life won the victory and Death was swallowed up.
This was written in the scriptures how one Death consumed the other,
And thus made a mockery of Death. Hallelujah!

Here is the true Passover Lamb, God had commanded it.
High upon the cross's shaft it has been roasted in ardent love.
The blood marks our doors, faith holds it before Death.
The evil one can no longer harm us. Hallelujah!

So we celebrate the high feast with heartfelt joy and delight.
That the Lord lets shine for us, He is himself the sun
Who through the splendor of His grace lights up our hearts completely,
The night of sin has disappeared. Hallelujah!

We eat and live well with the true unleavened bread of Easter.
The old leaven shall not be with the Word of grace.
Christ would be the meal and would feed the soul only,
Faith wants no other life. Hallelujah!

Here are two distinct stories, but it was one and the same God who brought both Israel out of Egypt and Jesus out of the tomb. We as Christians belong to both stories and by them we are set free and wondrously fed. Alleluia!

Come, You Faithful, Raise the Strain

WORDS: John of Damascus, c.696-c.754, tr. John M. Neale, 1818-1866, alt.
MUSIC: Bohemian Brethren's *Gesangbuch,* 1544

7.6.7.6.D
Ave Virgo Virginum

The Day of Resurrection!

WORDS: John of Damascus, c.696-c.754, tr. John M. Neale, 1818-1866, alt.
MUSIC: Henry T. Smart, 1813-1879

7.6.7.6.D
Lancashire

"After becoming acquainted with the quaintness of the melody in singing the first stanza, we felt the power of the text and music mounting.
As we sang the last stanza, tears were running down our cheeks. We laughed, clapped, and shouted our approval, prophesying that this would surely become one of the most loved hymns in the new hymnal."

Sing It Again

With the death of J. Irving Erickson in 1992, an enormous loss was suffered in the history and interpretation of Covenant hymnody. As yet, no one with his knowledge, skill and dedication has risen to fill the vacuum left by his passing. I carry with me two "snapshots" of J. Irving that I will always cherish.

The first is from the early 1970s when the hymnal commission was nearing the completion of its work on what is now called the "red" hymnal. On this occasion we met in the lounge of First Covenant Church, Minneapolis. As the meeting got underway, J. Irving, as chairman of the commission, distributed sheets of a Swedish hymn, recently translated for the North Park College Choir by Karl Olsson. None of us were familiar with the hymn. J. Irving explained that it came from a Swedish Moravian hymnody popular in the mid-1700s, a full century before the music of the 1800s Awakening, more familiar to Covenanters. I recall standing and singing this "new" hymn with the members of the commission as J. Irving led us:

> O let your soul now be filled with gladness,
> Your heart redeemed, rejoice indeed!
> O may the thought banish all your sadness
> That in his blood you have been freed.

After becoming acquainted with the quaintness of the melody in singing the first stanza, we felt the power of the text and music mounting. As we sang the last stanza, tears were running down our cheeks. We laughed, clapped, and shouted our approval, prophesying that this would surely become one of the most loved hymns in the new hymnal. That prophesy has come true, thanks to J. Irving, Karl Olsson, Royce Eckhardt—the arranger—and the Swedish Moravians of the 18th century!

My second J. Irving "snapshot" is quite different. He was our consultant, an elder statesman, for the latest Covenant hymnal commission. In this role, he often reminded us that as the other Scandinavian-American denominations merged or simply lost touch with their heritage, the Evangelical Covenant had become the primary custodian of Scandinavian hymnody in North America. Without the Covenant, it could easily be lost altogether. But beyond that, he would offer advice only when asked. Even after his death, we members of the commission knew—with a high degree of certainty—what Irving would think and even how he would vote!

The one exception to his more passive role occurred in his last meeting with us held at the Winnetka Covenant Church, Chicago, in the autumn of 1992. The old gospel song, "I Surrender All," had been submitted for possible inclusion in the new hymnal. A lengthy discussion followed. Some recalled it from the days of the old "brown" hymnal (published 1931); others spoke favorably of it as one of the better songs in the gospel hymn tradition. Finally, J. Irving could restrain himself no longer. With face flushed and emotion in his voice, he said with all the force he could muster, "When we sing in church of all places, let us be honest! This hymn tends to make liars of us all, including me. Who of us can sing with all honesty, 'I surrender all'?" It could be argued that the hymn is more a statement of aspiration—as many of our hymns are—rather than a statement of fact, but after J. Irving's passionate argument, a vote was taken and the hymn was promptly rejected.

There, two snapshots of a great hymnologist: one pleading for honesty in what we sing; the other celebrating a gladness without ending and an all-inclusive grace "That by his death he has opened heaven, that you are ransomed as you are."

Beside such grace in Christ's perfect self-surrender, both by his life and death, our claims to special holiness seem small, if not trivial indeed!

(In respect for J. Irving's position, we are not republishing "I Surrender All" in this volume. However, you can find it printed in the "brown" Covenant hymnal of 1931 as hymn 192.)

O Let Your Soul Now Be Filled with Gladness
1 O let your soul now be filled with glad-ness, your heart re-deemed, re - joice in - deed! O may the thought ban - ish all your sad - ness that in his blood you have been freed, that God's un - fail - ing love is yours, that you the on - ly Son were giv - en, that by his
2 If you seem emp - ty of an - y feel - ing, re-joice— you are his ran-somed bride! If those you cher - ish seem not to love you, and dark as - sails from ev - 'ry side, still yours the prom-ise, come what may, in loss and tri-umph, in laugh-ter, cry - ing, in want and
3 It is a good ev-'ry good tran-scend-ing that Christ has died for you and me! It is a glad - ness that has no end - ing there- in God's won-drous love to see! Praise be to you, O spot-less Lamb, who through the des - ert my soul are lead - ing to that fair

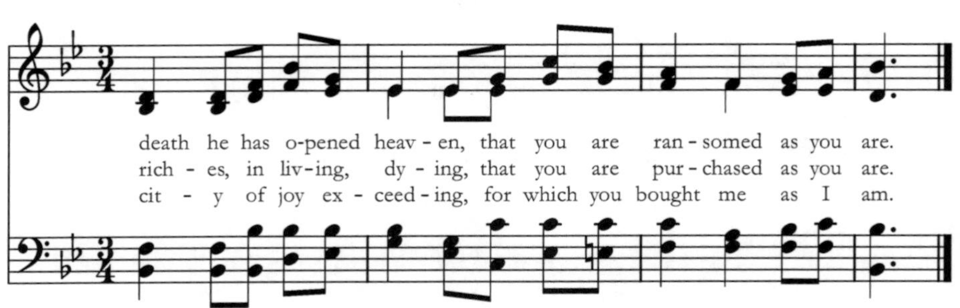

WORDS: Peter Jonsson Aschan, 1726-1813, tr. Karl A. Olsson, 1913-1996, 10.8.10.8.8.10.10.8

Ransomed Soul
MUSIC: Swedish melody; arr. A. Royce Eckhardt, 1937-,

The Feast is Waiting

In an unforgettable series of lectures on the saints, based on Saint Augustine's "Steps of Wisdom," given at an East Coast Ashram in 1953, Eric Hawkinson, then dean of North Park Seminary, concluded by dealing with a dimension in our Covenant heritage that I have seldom heard spoken of before or since—namely, ecstasy. "We have come out of ecstatic living," he said, "often hidden, but something in our forebears that never wore off."

As a boy growing up, I felt this ecstasy in certain first-generation "Mission Friends," as Covenanters were once called, and in my own grandfather, but it was seldom expressed communally. It happened to me, however, when my wife Jane and I were guests of the Annual Meeting of the Mission Covenant Church of Sweden in June, 1974. On the evening when a number of men and women were to be ordained, the new Immanuel Church in Stockholm was filled to the last seat. Unlike Americans, Swedes don't chatter when they enter the church. We all sat in perfect silence for thirty minutes. Then, an older man with a strong voice began singing a song by Nils Frykman, *"O sällhet stor"* (literally, "O bliss so great"). No hymn number was announced, but the congregation joined in spontaneously, singing all five verses by heart. It was truly a moment of ecstasy for me and one that has never worn off. I left the service that evening with a resolve to translate that song—if not for others, at least for myself.

Several months passed during which I struggled with how to express poetically the same ecstasy in the hymn that I had felt in the original. Translating is an arduous task. What happened next is one of those "aha" moments that might be called ecstatic. At the Covenant Midwinter Conference in 1976, held at the Northbrook Covenant Church, Chicago, I was greeted warmly, as always, by my dear friend of many years, Aaron Markuson, who took out of his coat pocket the translation of a song on which he had been working. "Here, Glen, take it and see what you can do with it." For me, it was another of those moments of ecstasy. "I can't believe it!" I exclaimed. "I've been working on the same song." It was Nils Frykman's song, "O sällhet stor," which Aaron had heard sung by the much-loved Swedish Gospel singer, Artur Erickson. So began our collaboration on "How Great the Joy."

For both of us there were some wrinkles in the text that we found difficult to iron out. In the second verse, for example, the literal translation of the last line is, "When the world's pleasure comes to an end we have the best wine still." The allusion, of course, is to the miracle at Cana of Galilee where Jesus turned the water into wine. Not only would many of the old Pietists, who were often also friends of temperance, demur in singing about being connoisseurs of fine wine, but also it presented an almost insurmountable problem for the translator. The resolution of that dilemma was not that far off. Thus, "When earthly pleasures reach their end our feast of joy will just begin."

The song first appeared in the silver supplement, *The Song Goes On*. When sung, it seemed to strike that note of ecstasy I felt in hearing it for the first time at Immanuel Church. This was something I had also felt in that first generation of Mission Friends I knew, and something I felt in meeting Aaron Markuson at Northbrook. My one objection—the same as Karl Olsson had voiced earlier about his translation of "O Let Your Soul Now Be Filled with Gladness"—is that people often sing it too fast. The text by Frykman is not one of triumphalism, as if ecstasy can somehow transcend hardship and travail. Rather, it is more like the bird singing through wind and storm. Or, like Eric Hawkinson quoting John Calvin: "Let us learn to be so delighted with Christ alone that the perception of his grace may overcome and at length remove from us all the distresses of the flesh." Or, in my own words, learn to see and take to heart in the bleakest moments the ultimate goodness and joy of being God's children and feel the need to praise and sing "Hallelujah!" Whatever tensions we may feel between the trials and hardships of the earthly journey and the Christian hope, Frykman's song helps us feel ecstasy, if not now in its fullness, then in the bridal feast that is waiting.

> With joy we walk with Jesus here, how great a Friend is he!
> But think what joy awaits us there, when heaven's light we see.
> Our hopes and dreams will be complete, when at the heav'nly feast we meet.
> Hallelujah, hallelujah, hallelujah, amen!"

How Great the Joy

WORDS: Nils Frykman, 1842-1911, tr. Aaron Markuson, 1910-2010, Glen V. Wiberg, 1925-

MUSIC: Engelke's *Lofsånger*

8.6.8.6.8.8.
with Refrain
Day of Redemption

A Magic Moment

One of the magic moments of our Scandinavian Holiday Tour, led by Eloise and LeRoy Nelson, was a visit to Fröderyd, a small, rural community located in the deep forests of the Swedish province of Småland, the birthplace of Lina Sandell. Most magic moments are unplanned, full of surprise, and always more than we could ever imagine. Few of us were prepared for the warm reception given us by our host, Nils Liedholm, or by the women of this rural Lutheran parish. Places at tables with fresh flowers and lovely china were set for us, thirty-five American guests. Our host, Nils, in the best English he could muster, earnestly told us the story of Lina Sandell (1832-1903). Then our hostess, Gun Lanka, served coffee, freshly-baked cardamom rolls, and cookies.

Afterwards, we visited Sandell's childhood home, her father's parsonage. Jonas Sandell was the much-loved pastor of the parish. Each room in the home spoke of piety and simplicity. Behind the parsonage was the 250-year-old ash tree under which she composed many of her hymns and poems. Nils Liedholm indicated that a recent discovery of more of her hymns brings the total to some 2,500! In our present hymnal, we have 11 of them. Perhaps the most frequently sung are "Children of the Heavenly Father," "Day by Day and with Each Passing Moment," "Thy Holy Wings Dear Savior," "Great Hills May Tremble," and "Thou Tender, Gracious Father."

The magic moment occurred after we crossed the country road to enter this impressive parish church—now restored after a devastating fire some years ago. It was inevitable before we left that we sang her most-loved hymn, "Children of the Heavenly Father." In the balcony, Marlyce Peterson played the organ and I sat at the piano below as 35 American voices joined in singing the first verse in Swedish and the remainder in English. There were few dry eyes as we left the sanctuary that morning.

A light rain was falling. But before leaving for the bus, I needed to search out the final resting place in the church yard of Lina's father, Jonas Sandell. Lina, at 26 years of age, had been accompanying her father on a boat trip across Lake Vättern when, as he stood by the railing, the boat gave a sudden lurch, throwing him overboard to his death. This tragedy brought deep and continuing grief to Lina, but also gave us some of her greatest and most popular hymns. When I found the small, black stone monolith, I knelt in thanksgiving to God for what Jonas and Fredrica had given to the world in their daughter, Lina.

Beyond the personal and private moments of reflection, our visit must have been newsworthy! A reporter from the local newspaper was sent to cover our visit. He interviewed several of us, especially those whose forebears had come from Småland. Later, Eloise sent us a copy of the paper with a picture of our group, a rather lengthy description of those interviewed, and an account of our singing of the first verse of *"Tryggare kan ingen vara."* The reporter wrote that we sang in *"klingande Svenska"* (literally, "ringing Swedish"). Our hostess, Gun Lanka, said that our visit would go down in her daybook as the highlight of her summer. And for us—a magic time indeed!

Children of the Heavenly Father

WORDS: Lina Sandell, 1832-1903, tr. Ernst W. Olson, 1870-1958,

MUSIC: Swedish melody, 1874

8.8.8.8
Tryggare Kan Ingen Vara

God the Nurturer

In pursuing a favorite pastime of reading through hymnals, I have often wondered why so few of our Swedish heritage hymns are included in American hymnals. Several mainline denominations' hymnals have included two, "Children of the Heavenly Father" and "How Great Thou Art."

While the *Lutheran Book of Worship* has several Swedish chorales, the only representations of the pietistic heritage are the two above hymns and "With God as Our Friend" by Carl O. Rosenius and Oscar Ahnfelt. For many former Augustana Lutherans, the omission of more Swedish pietistic hymns from the *Lutheran Book of Worship* (1978) was a source of great unhappiness, if not also the shedding of tears. The supplement song book, *With One Voice,* has included two additional heritage hymns by Lina Sandell, a new translation of "Day by Day" and "Thy Holy Wings," translated by my good friend and teacher at Luther Seminary, Gracia Grindal. She made an interesting adaptation for the baptism of a newborn in her family, "Oh, wash me in the waters of Noah's cleansing flood," as I mentioned earlier.

This raises the issue of not simply tinkering around the edges of a hymn (which I suppose every hymnal commission or hymnologist has done over the centuries), but of a full scale reconstruction of an old hymn and its translation. Case in point: *The New Century Hymnal* (1995), the new hymnal and worship book of the United Church of Christ. Surprisingly, the two popular hymns mentioned above are included, with a total reconstruction of "Children of the Heavenly Father" and a re-translated version of "How Great Thou Art," newly titled "O Mighty God." Does that title have a familiar ring to people who remember the Covenant's "red" hymnal of 1973? Many readers may have some interest in what has happened to two hymns so firmly entrenched in our memory banks and singing tradition. In the index to *The New Century Hymnal* one finds in italics "Children of the Heavenly Father" signaling a change in title to the more accurate translation "Surely No One Can Be Safer" *("Tryggare kan ingen vara").*

The New Century Hymnal

Surely no one can be safer
Than God's children held in favor,
Not the stars so brightly burning,
Not the birds to nests returning.

With the flock God is abiding,
Heaven's plenty all providing,
Rich in mercy, never sparing,
Like a father, gently caring.

None shall ever meet rejection,
Be denied God's own protection;
Has there been a friend who better
Knows our hopes, our fears that fetter?

(Verse 4 has been eliminated)

Whether taking, whether giving
God alone remains forgiving,
And with one true purpose holy
To preserve our welfare solely.

The Covenant Hymnal

Children of the heavenly Father
Safely in his bosom gather
Nestling bird nor star in heaven
Such a refuge e'er was given.

God his own doth tend and nourish,
In his holy courts they flourish;
From all evil things he spares them,
In his mighty arms he bears them.

Neither life nor death shall ever
From the Lord his children sever;
Unto them his grace he showeth,
And their sorrows all he knoweth.

Praise the Lord in joyful numbers,
Your Protector never slumbers;
At the will of your Defender
Ev'ry foeman must surrender.

Though he giveth or he taketh
God his children ne'er forsaketh;
His the lovely purpose solely
To preserve them pure and holy

The Swedish Psalmbook
Original by Lina Sandell

Tryggare kan ingen vara
Än Guds lilla barnaskara,
Stjärnan ej på himlafästet,
Fågeln ej i kända nästet.

Herren sina trogna vårdar
Uti Sions helga gårdar;
Över dem han sig förbarmar,
Bär dem uppå fadersarmar.

Ingen nöd och ingen lycka
Skall utur hans hand dem rycka.
Han, vår vän för andra vänner,
Sina barns bekymmer känner.

Gläd dig då du lilla skara:
Jakobs Gud skall dig bevara.
För hans vilja måste alla
Fiender till jorden falla.

Vad han tar och vad han giver,
Samme Fader han dock bliver,
Och hans mål är blott det ena:
Barnets sanna väl allena.

A literal, free verse translation
Mark Safstrom

Safer can no one be
Than God's little flock of children
Not the star in the firmament of heaven,
Not the bird in its familiar nest.

The Lord cares for his faithful ones
In the holy gardens of Zion;
Over them he grants his mercy,
Bears them on father's arms.

No distress and no stroke of fortune
Shall steal them from his hand.
He, our friend above all other friends,
Knows the cares of his children.

Rejoice, then, you little flock:
The God of Jacob shall preserve you.
Before his will must all
Enemies fall to the ground.

No matter what he takes, nor what he gives,
The same Father he will yet remain,
And his purpose is but this one:
Simply the true well-being of his child.

One must give the translator and *The New Century Hymnal* high marks for taking Sandell's hymn seriously. There is even a biographical statement beneath the hymn:

> Lina Sandell endured many hardships in her early years, including illness, the death of a child, and the drowning of her father who was a Swedish Lutheran pastor. She maintained a deep piety and strong commitment to mission, and wrote more than 650 hymns and poems. (Hymn 487.)

Singing the new translation among Covenanters would, no doubt, receive a cold reception, if not a hot protest. What have you done with the hymn we have sung at baptisms, weddings, funerals and numerous other occasions? Beyond the sentiment attached to the hymn or having the first verse of the Swedish text beneath it, what might make this new translation unacceptable to a Covenanter?

While in some ways, this translation is closer to the original, it seems more distant, lacking in warmth. The emphasis of the hymn, as we sing it, is on God's embrace and nurture more than safety. (It is placed in our new hymnal under the category of "God the Nurturer.") The lovely image of "safely in his bosom gather" becomes "held in his favor."

Further, "Neither life nor death shall ever from the Lord his children sever" gives way to abstract doctrine, "None shall ever meet rejection, be denied God's own protection." In the same verse "their sorrows all he knoweth" becomes a question: "Has there been a friend who better knows our hopes, our fears that fetter?" It seems to me that the evocative imagery of the God who knows all our sorrows has greater power to comfort, especially when standing at the edge of the grave, than simply a question about one who knows our hopes and fears.

When the late Erik Routley lectured on hymnody at North Park Theological Seminary in Chicago in the spring of 1979, I asked what his evaluation of the hymn "Children of the Heavenly Father" might be. He quickly responded, "I think it might be sung too often among your people." The value of a new translation, even if it cannot replace the old, is to make us more aware of what we may be singing too often and thoughtlessly. In using a new translation of this hymn, however, we lose some of the emotional weight that the traditional English translation carries—emotional weight closer to the power of what Lina Sandell wrote while seated on the branch of a large ash tree in the backyard of the parsonage at Fröderyd, Sweden. What moved her to write is still what moves us—knowing God as a loving father, embracing, shielding, and carrying his children in his arms.

More Secure Is No One Ever

WORDS: Lina Sandell, 1832-1903, tr. Composite
MUSIC: Swedish melody, 1874

8.8.8.8
Tryggare Kan Ingen Vara

Tryggare Kan Ingen Vara

WORDS: Lina Sandell, 1832-1903
MUSIC: Swedish melody, 1874

L.M.
Tryggare Kan Ingen Vara

"I told them to read Caedmon's Hymn,
remembering how they had felt when they sang,
and to consider the possibility that
these people of 1500 years ago felt many of
the same emotions we do."

Architect of Creation

Kit Swanson, a Peace Corps volunteer teaching in a university in Cameroon, West Africa, once taught a course in Old English Literature. In a letter to her parents, Dave and Ann Swanson of the Bethlehem Covenant Church, Kit describes her class of more than 200 students and "a sighting in Christian music" that is quite remarkable. She writes:

> While we were waiting for the department head to help us out, I wrote Caedmon's Hymn on the chalkboard. (Caedmon's hymn is one of the oldest of English poems, written between 658 and 680.) All 200-plus dutiful and obedient young Cameroonians automatically copied it into their notebooks. No one had asked them to do that... I gave the class about five minutes on the history of England around 500 AD. Then I asked if the students knew "How Great Thou Art." They did and they began to sing. First a timid voice or two, then a strong one. Within a few seconds there were 200-plus voices singing perfect four-part harmony. It was truly awesome. They were cheers and loud applause at the end. I told them to read Caedmon's Hymn, remembering how they had felt when they sang, and to consider the possibility that these people of 1500 years ago felt many of the same emotions we do. The lead instructor said: "I can see this is going to be an experience."

Dave Swanson was curious about this ancient hymn and asked for help from a most knowledgeable source, Flora Sedgwick, a retired teacher of English Literature from Minnehaha Academy and an active member of the Bethlehem Church, both in Minneapolis. Not only did she know of Caedmon's Hymn but also numerous literary sources on the Anglo-Saxon period, including the story told by Venerable Bede of how Caedmon composed the hymn. The literal translation is as follows:

> Now we must praise heaven-kingdom's Guardian,
> The Creator's might and his mind plans,
> The work of the Glory-Father,
> Then he of wonders of every one,
> Eternal Lord, the beginning established.
> He first created for men's sons
> Heaven as a roof, holy Creator:
> Then middle-earth, mankind's Guardian
> Eternal Lord, afterwards made
> For men earth, Master almighty.

The Venerable Bede, the great cleric of Old England, tells the story of its composition in his *Ecclesiastical History of the English People.* Shy of singing in public, Caedmon always found an excuse to avoid taking the harp and singing. One night when he left the feast table, he fell asleep in the stable where he had gone to tend the animals. As he slept, he had a dream that someone came to him and said, "Caedmon, sing me something." He sought, as always, to excuse himself, but the other insisted that he sing and told him to celebrate the beginning of created things. Caedmon at once sang the hymn and, upon waking, remembered the verses. Bede then goes on to report that from that dream on Caedmon became a monk and devoted his life to Christian verse and hymnody.

While it's wonderful to think of those African students singing a hymn from our heritage, it is also awesome to think of the connections Kit Swanson drew between Caedmon's hymn and Carl Boberg's *"O Store Gud"* ("O Mighty God"), spanning 1500 years and two continents. Boberg's hymn was inspired not by a dream. Rather, upon returning home from a Sunday service, he was enraptured watching a summer afternoon's thunderstorm sweep the horizon with flashes of lightning and loud crashes of thunder. Then, in the Sabbath stillness that followed—a rainbow. One wonders what this Mission Friend preacher would think about the world-wide popularity of his hymn. Perhaps he would feel many of the same emotions Caedmon felt or those African students felt or how countless numbers of people in our times still feel when singing his hymn, so similar to the themes of the hymn in Old English:

> O mighty God, when I behold the wonder
> Of nature's beauty, wrought by words of thine,
> And how thou leadest all from realms up yonder,
> Sustaining earthly life with love benign,
> With rapture filled, my soul thy name would laud,
> O mighty God! O mighty God!

—Translation by E. Gustav Johnson, *The Covenant Hymnal,* 1973

How Great Thou Art

WORDS: Carl Boberg, 1859-1940, para. Stuart K. Hine, 1899-1989 alt.,
© 1953, 1981 Manna Music, Inc.
MUSIC: Swedish melody; arr. Stuart K. Hine, 1899-1989,
© 1953, 1981 Manna Music, Inc.

11.10.11.10 with Refrain
O Store Gud

Our Mighty God Works Mighty Wonders

WORDS: Nils Frykman, 1842-1911, tr. A. L. Skoog, 1856-1934, Andrew T. Frykman, 1875-1943, alt. 9.8.9.8.8.8
MUSIC: Swedish melody Celebration

Surveying the Wonder

The popularity of "How Great Thou Art"—even on the fringes of American religious culture—must surely be due to its repeated use over the years in the Billy Graham Crusades, sung by George Beverly Shea. In *The Covenant Hymnal* (1973), the concluding sentence in the footnote of "O Mighty God, when I Behold the Wonder" (Hymn 19) tells its convoluted history, "The text widely known as *How Great Thou Art* is an English translation of a Russian version based on an earlier German translation of the original."

A helpful innovation in *The New Century Hymnal* (1995) of the United Church of Christ is the footnote with each hymn. For this hymn and its new translation "O Mighty God When I Survey in Wonder" (Hymn 35), the footnote tells the story in greater detail:

> Carl Boberg, a popular evangelical minister and teacher in Sweden, wrote his poem "O Store Gud" in the summer of 1885. Several years later he was surprised to hear it sung with this old Swedish melody, with which it has been associated ever since. The first literal English translation by E. Gustav Johnson was published in the United States in 1925. The hymn also became known in Germany and Russia, where the British missionary, Stuart K. Hine, was inspired to create his English paraphrase known as "How Great Thou Art."

Someone on that commission must have been blessed with a working knowledge of Swedish!

Further, it is likewise praiseworthy that Carl Boberg, who was a well-known preacher in the Mission Covenant Church of Sweden, is given recognition as the author of the hymn and E. Gustav Johnson as its first English translator. Our first three Covenant Hymnals in English used his translation and *The Covenant Hymnal* (1973) included all nine verses of Boberg's original poem, first published in a Swedish religious newspaper on March 23, 1886.

Given the popularity of Stuart Hine's translation of "How Great Thou Art" in the late 1960s and early 1970s, the Covenant's hymnal commission struggled with whether to go with the more popular version or retain E. Gustav Johnson's translation. However, economics settled the issue, inasmuch as we were unable to pay the exorbitant price requested by the publishing house that owned the copyright despite the fact that the original belonged to the Covenant. One of the ironies of music making and profiteering!

In *The Covenant Hymnal—A Worshipbook* (1996), the more popular translation by Stuart Hines has replaced E. Gustav Johnson's version which, while closer to the original, uses more archaic language. While there was sympathy on the commission for retaining this older version, a compromise led to preserving it in printed form on the opposite page of "How Great Thou Art." The newer version, with fresher language and some striking metaphors, seems uneven and incomplete.

The refrain of the Boberg's original text *"O Store Gud"* begins with a critical "then" as culmination to "when" at the beginning of each verse. ("O mighty God, when...") All three translations follow the original use of "when" with the exception of verse 3 in *The New Century Hymnal.* But only Hine's version uses "then" as the critical first word in the refrain "Then sings my soul, my Savior God to thee...." The "when" followed in the refrain by "then" is the most powerful poetic device in Boberg's entire text.

E. Gustav Johnson's refrain: "With rapture filled, my soul thy name would laud" and *The New Century Hymnal*'s "My soul cries out in praise to you" are closer to the original *"Då brister själen uti lovsångsljud..."* The word *"brister"* is a very strong word suggesting a breaking out of the soul in praise and compared to the other two translations, Hine's refrain "Then sings my soul, my Savior, God to Thee..." seems a bit too tranquil, if not too tame.

Only *The New Century Hymnal* follows the original text by adding a final refrain: "Then we will sing your praise forevermore..." However, in the Swedish text, the soul's song of praise which opened the hymn *"O Store Gud"* ("O mighty God...") and which is repeated at the end of each stanza becomes in the final refrain, *"Tack, gode Gud"* ("Thanks, good God!"). The wonder and awe evoked in the soul of the singer at the prospect of eternal bliss is transformed at the hymn's conclusion into a familiar Swedish phrase which I often heard in immigrant prayers *"Tack, gode Gud."* It is unfortunate that none of the translators included this final word of thanks.

The late Eric Routley, eminent hymnologist, disliked both the hymn and its melody with vehemence. Ironically, as chief editor of the hymnal of the Reformed Church in America, he was forced to respond to the clamor of its members to include the hymn. He did so by writing a new text of "O mighty God" and re-harmonizing the Swedish tune. This was one of his last works, included in the Reformed Church's hymnal, *Rejoice in the Lord* (1985), as Hymn 466.

Following the torturous path translators have taken with a hymn such as "How Great Thou Art," we are reminded again of the immense task involved in translation. But even more, despite the changes to the original, the song has survived and continues to bless those standing in awe at the wondrous deeds of this mighty God. But I have a hunch that from some higher balcony, Carl Boberg looks down smiling at the stir he created for translators—all from a summer's afternoon walk beside a lake and through the woods in a thunderstorm. Then I can almost see him folding his hands and saying *"Tack, gode Gud!"* "Thanks, good God!"

The Covenant Hymnal (1973)

O mighty God, when I behold the wonder
Of nature's beauty, wrought by words of thine,
And how thou leadest all from realms up yonder,
Sustaining earthly life with love benign,

Refrain:
With rapture filled, my soul thy name would laud,
O mighty God! O mighty God! *(repeat)*

When I behold the heavens in their vastness,
Where golden ships in azure issue forth,
Where sun and moon keep watch upon the fastness
Of changing seasons and of time on earth.

When crushed by guilt of sin before thee kneeling,
I plead for mercy and for grace and peace,
I feel thy balm and, all my bruises healing,
My soul is filled, my heart is set at ease.

And when at last the mists of time have vanished
And I in truth my faith confirmed shall see,
Upon the shores where earthly ills are banished
I'll enter Lord, to dwell in peace with thee.

—Selected verses from Hymn 19
Words: Carl Boberg, 1859-1940, tr. E. Gustav Johnson, 1893-1974,

O Store Gud!

As published in 1894 in "I Moll och Dur," *a collection of Carl Boberg's poems*

O store Gud, när jag den värld beskådar,
Som du har skapat med ditt allmaktsord,
Hur där din visdom leder lifvets trådar
Och alla väsen mätas vid ditt bord;

Refrain:
Då brister själen ut i lofsångsljud:
O store Gud! O store Gud!

När jag betraktar himlens höga under,
Där gyllne världsskepp plöja etern blå,
Och sol och måne mäta tidens stunder
Och växla om, som tvänne klockor gå;

När jag hör åskans röst i stormen brusa
Och blixtens klingor springa fram ur skyn,
När regnets kalla, friska skurar susa
Och löftets båge glänser för min syn;

När sommarvinden susar öfver fälten,
När blommor dofta omkring källans strand,
När trastar drilla i de gröna tälten
Vid furuskogens tysta, dunkla rand;

När jag i bibeln skåda alla under,
Som Herren gjort se'n förste Adams tid,
Hur nådefull han varit alla stunder
Och hjälpt sitt folk ur lifvets synd och strid;

När jag hör dårar i sin dårskaps dimma
Förneka Gud och håna, hvad han sagt,
Men ser likväl, att de hans hjälp förnimma
Och uppehållas af hans nåd och makt;

Och när jag ser hans bild till jorden sväfva
Och göra väl och hjälpa öfverallt,
När jag ser satan fly och döden bäfva
För Herren i förklarad korsgestalt;

När tryckt af syndens skuld jag faller neder
Vid Herrens fot och ber om nåd och frid,
Och han min själ på rätta vägen leder
Och frälsar mig från all min synd och strid;

När slutligt alla tidens höljen falla
Och i åskådning byter sig min tro
Och evighetens klara klockor kalla
Min frälsta ande till dess sabbatsro;

Då brister själen ut i lofsångsljud:
Tack gode Gud! Tack gode Gud!

A literal, free verse translation
Mark Safstrom

O, great God, when I survey the world,
Which you have made with your almighty word,
How your wisdom leads all the threads of life there
And all of existence is fed at your table;

Refrain (for all but the last verse):
Then my soul bursts out in the sound of songs of praise:
O, great God! O, great God!

When I survey the lofty wonders of the heavens,
Where golden planet-ships plow the eternal blue,
And sun and moon count the hours of time,
And change, just as two clocks would tick;

When I hear the voice of thunder roar within the storm
And swords of lightning leap forth from the sky,
When the cold, fresh rain swells rustle
And the Bow of Promise shines before my sight;

When the summer wind rustles over the field,
When flowers' fragrance floats along the banks of the spring,
When thrushes warble inside their green tents
At the quiet, dark edge of the pine forest;

When I observe all the wonders,
That the Lord has made since the first age of Adam,
How full of grace he has been at all times
And helped his people out of sin and the battles of life;

When I hear fools in the haze of their folly
Deny God and mock what he has said,
But then observe when they, too, realize his aid
And are upheld by his grace and power;

And when I see his image come descending to the earth,
Doing good works and giving aid in all things,
When I see Satan flee and death cower
Before the Lord, transfigured by the cross;

When crushed by debt of sin I fall down
At the foot of the Lord and pray for grace and peace,
And he leads my soul in right paths
And delivers me from all my sin and strife;

When at last all the veils of time fall
And in reflection, my faith is exchanged for this sight
And the clear bells of eternity call
My ransomed soul to its Sabbath peace;

Refrain (last verse):
Then my soul will burst out in the sound of songs of praise:
Thank you, good God! Thank you, good God

The New Century Hymnal

O mighty God, when I survey in wonder
The World that formed when once the word you said,
The strands of life all woven close together,
The whole creation at your table fed,

Refrain (verses 1-3):
My soul cries out in songs of praise to you,
O mighty God! O mighty God! *(repeat)*

When your voice speaks in rolls of thunder pealing,
Your lightning power bursts in bright surprise;
When cooling rain, your gentle love revealing,
Reflects your promise, arcing through the skies.
The Bible tells the story of your blessing
So freely shed upon all human life;
Your constant mercy, every care addressing,
relieving burdened souls from sin and strife.

And when at last, the clouds of doubt dispersing,
You will reveal what we but dimly see;
With trumpet call, our great rebirth announcing,
We shall rejoin you for eternity.

Refrain (verse 4):
Then we will sing your praise forever more,
O mighty God! O mighty God! *(repeat)*

—*New Century Hymnal,* Pilgrim Press, Cleveland, Ohio, Hymn 35.

A Costly Sacrifice

"Blood in the hymnal" seems an odd theme to pursue—until you encounter a person with furrowed brow (or someone with tongue-in-cheek) asking a member of a hymnal commission, "Have you taken *the blood* out of the hymnal?" Given the near earth-shaking significance in the history of the Covenant Church and the doctrinal struggles surrounding the definition of atonement theology in the 1870s, it is not a question that should be passed over lightly or answered in a defensive manner.

In most cases, the one who asks the question seriously feels there has been a conspiracy afoot by a hymnal commission to exclude "Power in the Blood" or "Are You Washed in the Blood?" or "Nothing but the Blood of Jesus" from the canon of the hymnal. Rarely indeed is the hymn, "There is a Fountain Filled with Blood," found in newer hymnals because the images seem to many to be overstated and downright offensive. But even here, the exceptions to such cases are noteworthy. In the recent Lutheran hymnal for African-American congregations, *This Far by Faith* (1999), nearly all such Gospel hymns coming out of 19th century American revivalism with blood imagery are included. Perhaps this represents a prophetic protest to a white, middle-class fixation on propriety and good taste, which would remove from the hymnody of the church the offense of what, in most cases, is solid Biblical material in both Old and New Testaments.

The pietistic revival movement of 19th-century Sweden borrowed many hymns from the Moravians. While the older Lutheran piety emphasized in its hymnody the themes of sin, repentance, and a struggle for holiness, Moravian piety was characterized by songs of joy, triumph, peace and blessing given in the Crucified. But the blood-imagery, according to Karl Olsson, could be downright ghoulish—for example, the hymn mentioned earlier in which believers were described as blood-worms in the wounds of Jesus.

One of the Moravian hymns that has survived in all of the Covenant hymnals over the past hundred years is "My Crucified Savior" (in Swedish, *"Min blodige Konung,"* meaning "My bloody King"). See *The Covenant Hymnal: A Worshipbook,* Hymn 236. The second stanza, where the original stated the old satisfaction theory of the atonement, speaking of the Savior as having *"appeased the Creator* and mankind restored," the word "appeased" was changed to "obeyed," thus bringing it into line with traditional Covenant theology.

Finer examples of this Moravian hymnody are contained in "O Let Your Soul Now Be Filled with Gladness" (Hymn 494), in which the Savior's blood has brought us freedom, unending gladness, and the unfailing love of God and, thereby banished sadness, even in the most trying circumstances. Also, the Moravian emphasis on the blood of Christ is the theme of another hymn that is both strong and joyful as a confession of faith:

> If asked whereon I rest my claim to full salvation's joy,
> If nothing more I need to name or other words employ
> Besides our Savior's blood and wounds, to me all satisfying grounds,
> I answer then, "My claim is good! 'Tis based on Jesus' blood." (Hymn 353)

If those of us who consider ourselves Covenanters have learned anything from the definition of the atonement advanced by our theological leader, Paul Peter Waldenström, it should be that Jesus' blood is not a magic "stain remover" that makes God gracious, but is instead the following:

> But what is meant then with the expression the blood of Jesus? Blood and life are closely related. Already in the Old Testament it is stated; in Lev. 17:11 we read in the original text: *"The life of the body is in the blood,* and I have given it to you to shed on the altar, so that your lives might be reconciled thereby, *for blood reconciles through the life that it makes possible."* [...] From these words we understand that blood is an expression which means life, and this understanding immediately sheds a beautiful, heavenly light on the words of the scriptures about the blood of Jesus. (Waldenström, recounted by Axel Andersson 1931, *Den Kristna Försoningsläran efter P. Waldenström.* p. 23).

Then he adds that the life sacrificed on the cross is the means of our participation in that same sacrifice, thereby bringing about change in us.

There is much more about blood in the hymnal, but meanwhile the offense stands. In an era when church marketing and church growth strategies would have us distance ourselves from any hint of suffering, death, the cross, the blood, or even the sacraments if we are to be "successful" evangelists, we need more than ever in "psalms, hymns and spiritual songs" to sing praise to God for the blood, the life laid down and life restored that has revealed this wondrous love which has redeemed us and made us His people.

"Amazing love! How can it be that thou, my God, shouldst die for me?"

If Asked Whereon I Rest My Claim

WORDS: *Brödraförsamlingen,* Copenhagen, 1748, tr. A. Samuel Wallgren, 1885-1940
MUSIC: Swedish melody, *Zions Nya Sånger,* 1874

8.6.8.6.8.8.8.6
Salighetsgrund

And Can It Be That I Should Gain

WORDS: Charles Wesley, 1707-1788
MUSIC: Thomas Campbell, 1777-1844

L.M.D.
Sagina

A Nobler Theme

In the last essay, I spoke of the imagery of blood in Covenant hymnody and how it reflects the centrality of the atoning death of Jesus in our theology. While the Covenant's hymnal commission did not include the hymn by William Cowper, "There is a Fountain Filled with Blood," it wasn't because it isn't a good hymn nor because it's bloodthirsty, but because in a literal-minded culture like ours, it could be misunderstood by many people who would be repulsed by the very thing they need most. I share my regret with author Kathleen Norris that, in losing this hymn, we will not get to sing "Redeeming love has been my theme, and shall be 'til I die," which continues in the last verse:

> Then in a nobler, sweeter song I'll sing Thy power to save,
> When this poor lisping stammering tongue
> Lies silent in the grave.

It is interesting, however, that devotional hymns contemplating the passion of Jesus, while laden with emotion and images of blood, do not evoke feelings of revulsion or violate the sense of good taste. Rather, the best of these meditative hymns address the saving event of Jesus' death as the transforming, renewing, and sanctifying work of God in the minds and hearts of believers.

In the Lutheran tradition, Paul Gerhardt's (1607-1676) striking and graphic hymn of the Passion is sung with awe and often with tears during Holy Week:

> O sacred Head now wounded, with grief and shame weighed down,
> Now scornfully surrounded with thorns, thy only crown.
> How art thou pale with anguish, with sore abuse and scorn!
> How does that visage languish which once was bright as morn!

Drawn into his pain and the anguish of his death, we fall prostrate in adoring wonder and sing:

> O make me thine forever, and, should I fainting be,
> Lord, let me never, never outlive my love to Thee.

In a similar way, the hymns of Isaac Watts (1674-1748) draw us into the Passion narrative in our reflecting on the unfolding drama. One of the most well-known of all the hymns of Lent must surely be "When I Survey the Wondrous Cross." The sense of time is transcended as the singer is transported to the sacred ground beneath the cross as a witness to his dying.

See, from his head, his hands, his feet,
Sorrow and love flow mingled down.
Did e'er such love and sorrow meet,
Or thorns compose so rich a crown?

In contemplating the wondrous cross, one can only be overwhelmed by "love so amazing, so divine," so that a liberating and transforming moment occurs in the heart of the believer.

All the vain things that charm me most,
I sacrifice them to his blood.

—*The Covenant Hymnal,* Hymn 222

"Alas! And Did My Savior Bleed" is another of Watts' hymns of the Passion that contemplates the great sacrifice with an appreciation for the inestimable cost. This is quite different from the early Swedish Moravian hymnody in which the wounds of Jesus are also praised:

Thou well of blessedness,
I open my mouth;
Let thy blood run
And I shall be content...
a single blood drop
Out of thy wounds
Stills my moan,
And calms my suffering.

—*Songs of Moses and the Lamb, 1839*

Whereas lines need to be drawn at hymns speaking of a fountain filled with blood or blood dripping from open wounds, I would assess the range of our hymns drawing on blood imagery to be too limited by their subjectivity. Even in the finest of our devotional hymns of the Passion, it is so easy to narrow Jesus down to our Jesus, to our experience, to our way of knowing—thereby missing the cosmic significance of his atoning death. What is lacking in many of our Passion hymns is the strong, bracing tonic of the early hymn writer, Fortunatus (530-609), in his classic hymn, "Sing My Tongue." This hymn expresses the *Christus Victor* (Christ is Victor) theme, one of the earlier ideas about the atonement.

The human Jesus, blood and all, includes us in a cosmic redemption. Again, as Kathleen Norris says, "The rhythm of life that we carry in our veins is not only for us, but for others, as Christ's incarnation (and death) was for the sake of all."

Sing My Tongue, the Glorious Battle

6 Faithful cross, true sign of triumph,
be for all the noblest tree;
none in foliage, none in blossom,
none in fruit your equal be;
symbol of the world's redemption,
for your burden makes us free.

7 Unto God be praise and glory;
to the Father and the Son,
to the_eternal Spirit honor
now and evermore be done;
praise and glory in the highest,
while the timeless ages run. Amen.

WORDS: Venantius Honorius Fortunatus, 530-609; tr. John Mason Neale, 1818-1866, alt. — 8.7.8.7.8.7
MUSIC: Plainsong mode III, Vatican collection — Pange Lingua

At the Lamb's High Feast

WORDS: Office hymn, seventeenth century, tr. Robert Campbell, 1814-1868
MUSIC: *Bohemian Brethren's Kirchensänge,* 1566; arr. © 1969 Concordia Publishing House

7.7.7.7.4
Sonne Der Gerechtigkeit

With Many Voices

I recall from the earlier years of my ministry—when there were still some first-generation Swedes around—that whenever we sang a Swedish translation, someone was bound to say after the service, "It just isn't the same in the original." I felt the same response in Sweden when the congregation of Immanuel Church in Stockholm sang *"Dagen är kommen, kärlek triumferar,"* meaning "The day has come, love triumphs." This is the Swedish translation of the first line of "O Come, All Ye Faithful." A nice thought, but it just isn't the same as the original.

Having done a little translation of Swedish hymns, I know the problem of the translator, torn between being faithful to the literal meaning of the text and the challenge of matching words with music. I spent many months and not a few sleepless nights in my efforts at translating "Jesus of Nazareth Passes By." The first line of the original is *"Jesus från Nasaret går här fram,"* which translated literally is "Jesus from Nazareth here goes forth"—a bit more energetic than "passes by now as in ancient time" as I ended up translating it. My apologies to the hymn's author, a great hymn writer and priest in the Church of Sweden, Anders Frostenson!

In a chapel talk at North Park College some years ago, Wesley Nelson made reference to a much-loved hymn, "I Sing With Joy and Gladness" (Hymn 498). E. Gustav Johnson (1893-1974), who had translated Nils Frykman's text, was one of the finest translators of our heritage music. He taught English language and literature at both North Park Academy and College, as well as Swedish in the College. Though only ten of his translations are included in our present hymnal, there were 23 in the Hymnal of 1950. The second verse of the English version reads:

> My former resolution to lead a better life
> Were only vain delusions—my soul was still at strife:
> Now on the love of Jesus completely I rely
> For me he was willing to die.

In the chapel talk mentioned above, Nelson tells of discovering in Swedish the literal meaning of the second verse in the Frykman song.

> I formerly used to concentrate on repentance, prayer, and faith, but now I just concentrate on Jesus and his love for me.

What a translator's nightmare, but what a treasure of insight into Mission Friends theology and experience.

How bereft of the songs of our forebears we would be without the translations of E. Gustav Johnson or the little lady in the North Park Church in Chicago, Signe Bennett (1900-1996), who carried translations around in her heart and in a little brown book. She gave us another Frykman song, "The Highest Joy That Can Be Known" (Hymn 533), sung among our people for decades. She also translated, with me, the Mission Friends song, "O How Blest to be a Pilgrim" (Hymn 758).

But even more, think how much the poorer the whole English-speaking Church would be without the numerous translations of Catherine Winkworth (1827-1878), an English woman who went to live with her father in Germany. She mastered German and gave us great translations of German hymns such as "Now Thank We All Our God" (Hymn 31), "Praise to the Lord, the Almighty" (Hymn 61), "Jesus Priceless Treasure" (Hymn 459), and many other majestic hymns we would not want to live without.

At a hymn sing in which Martin Marty provided the commentary, he quoted—with tongue in cheek—from an Italian source that all translators are liars, meaning, most likely, that if you are going to sing or listen to an Italian opera or art song you should do so in the original language. Don't mess with translations, for those who try will end up as liars. But I propose that in our hymnody it is not a matter of lying or truth-telling or even being literal (which is almost impossible), but in catching the spirit of the song. Without the efforts of translators in whom the song lives, our English-language hymnody would be greatly impoverished!

Jesus of Nazareth Passes By

WORDS: Anders Frostenson, 1906-2006, tr. Glen V. Wiberg, 1925-,
© 1972, 1996 Covenant Publications
MUSIC: Gustaf L. Nordqvist, 1886-1949, © 1949 A.B. Nordiska Musikforlaget

9.6.9.6.7
Nordqvist

I Sing with Joy and Gladness

WORDS: Nils Frykman, 1842-1911, tr. E. Gustav Johnson, 1893-1974,

MUSIC: Nils Frykman, 1842-1911

13.13.13.8
Joyful Pilgrim

A Singer of Passion

I think it appropriate to pay tribute to the gospel singer, Winifred Larson, who was well known in many of our churches and whose passing was memorialized at First Evangelical Free Church of Minneapolis on May 16, 2003. The sanctuary was filled with a gathering of Free, Covenant, and Salvation Army folk who had come to honor the memory of a woman who sang and spoke in churches across America, Canada, and Sweden during her eighteen tours. From small congregations in northern Minnesota to Madison Square Garden, she touched the lives of many through song.

Sharing in the memorial service were two women who had been her accompanists in the later years of her 65 years of ministry, Frances Blomberg and Evelyn Dennison. They provided a medley of Winifred's favorite songs on the organ and piano. Most moving to me were the tributes by her niece, Kay Olson from the North Park Covenant Church in Chicago, and the fine baritone solo by Kay's husband, Don. He sang the song we had often heard her sing, "He the Pearly Gates Will Open," in both Swedish and English.

In the 1940s, Winifred Larson was often referred to as "the Kate Smith of the Gospel." (On one occasion, however, the Rev. A. J. Thorwall, an unforgettable Free Church evangelist, made the mistake of introducing her in special meetings as "the Mae West of the Gospel.") In the early 1940s, when I was about 14 years old, she came to my home church, First Covenant Church of Kansas City, and was a guest in our home. Winifred was the singer for a two-week series of evangelistic meetings conducted by a Free Church layman, C. B. Hedstrom, owner of the Hedstrom Shoe Store on North Clark Street in Chicago's "Andersonville." A successful shoe salesman and lay preacher, he was also the author of *Pay Day Some Day,* the story of his life—and the title of one of his sermons.

At the memorial service, the homily was given by an old friend of Winifred's, Dr. Lareau Lindquist, who characterized her as not an entertainer, but a soul-winner. That was her passion. But on at least one occasion, when she sang at Covenant Village Retirement Home, she failed to read her audience. After the concert, my mother invited Winifred, Jane, and me for coffee in her apartment. Reflecting on the evening, Winifred said: "I could see there was one worldly-looking woman under deep conviction as I sang and gave witness tonight." Interested to know who that might be, mother asked her to describe the woman and where she sat. That would be easy because she stood out in any crowd. "Oh, no," mother said, "That was the wife of a prominent Baptist minister in Minneapolis." No doubt, some of us clergy types and spouses may also need some further conversions.

Winifred's last concert took place at Bethany Home Village a few weeks after she had become a resident. Hearing that she had come from Florida to Bethany, I was eager to visit her, but saddened to see that a debilitating stroke had made communication nearly impossible. As I sat beside her in the lounge area, she showed signs of recognition. I told her stories of meeting her when I was 14, of playing piano for her one Sunday morning at the North Park Covenant Church when I was pastor. I reminded her of visits with my parents in Kansas City and later at Covenant Village. Because Winifred often accompanied herself with an autoharp, I brought mine along. The first song I heard her sing was her early signature song:

> I am a stranger here within a foreign land,
> My home is far away upon a golden strand.
> Ambassador to be in realms beyond the sea,
> I'm here on business for my King.
>
> *Refrain:*
> This is the message that I bring,
> A message angels feign would sing.
> "O be ye reconciled," thus says my Lord and King.
> "O be ye reconciled to me."

In song, the miracle happened. I sang the melody and to my surprise, she joined in with the alto, singing every word. Now people in the lounge began to gather around us, asking us to sing more. No audience was too small for her. That was her last concert, one that is a most cherished memory of my friend, Winifred Larson. And now the song goes on.

He the Pearly Gates Will Open

WORDS: Fredrik A. Blom; tr. Nathaniel Carlson
MUSIC: Alfred Olsen-Dulin, arr. Norman Johnson, arr.

Eternal Destiny
8.7.8.7. with refrain

Mercies Beyond Counting

Observances for Lina Sandell took place throughout 2003—on the centennial of her death—in our own country, in Scandinavia, and in many other places where her songs are known. A songfest honoring the life and work of Lina Sandell was held October 25, 2003 at Central Lutheran Church in Minneapolis and another the following evening at Luther Seminary in St. Paul. On November 9, a third songfest was held at the Salem Covenant Church in New Brighton for other Covenant churches in the area.

In the program notes at the Lutheran Reformation songfests, Gracia Grindal paid high tribute to the Covenant Church as "having been more persistent in keeping Sandell's legacy alive. Its hymnal includes 11 of her hymns in English," compared to only three in the *Lutheran Book of Worship* and the supplement *With One Voice.* This high tribute is due to the late J. Irving Erickson, who saw that part of the Covenant's calling is to preserve the music of our Scandinavian heritage.

In the early hymnal of the Augustana Lutheran Church, *Hemlandssånger ("Songs of the Homeland")* published in 1892, there were more than a 100 songs by Lina Sandell in a collection of 500 songs. The first official Covenant hymnal, *Sions Basun* ("Trumpet of Zion," 1908), included 60 of her songs. These statistics indicate that not all of her songs known and loved by Swedish immigrants have been preserved in translation. But it is interesting that in a recent poll, three of Sweden's ten most popular songs are by Sandell: "Children of the Heavenly Father," "Day by Day," and "Thy Holy Wings."

It may come as a surprise to some Covenant readers to learn that Lina Sandell, though a strong supporter and friend of the revival movement, did not belong to the Mission Covenant Church of Sweden. When the conflict broke out over the theology of its leader, Paul Peter Waldenström in 1872, Sandell was distressed by these controversies and wrote: "O, if we could only let everything go and hold more to the Lord." As a poet of the revival movement, she followed the traditional path charted by centuries of Pietists before her, choosing to remain within the state church of her country. She thus retained her membership in the national Church of Sweden, and evangelized from within in its revival wing, known as The Evangelical Homeland Foundation *(Evangeliska Fosterlands-Stiftelsen).* Nevertheless, Covenanters, along with others in the Lutheran, Evangelical Free Church, and other American churches, claim her as our own beloved sister in Christ.

Interestingly, the first exposure of Americans to the songs of Lina Sandell came in 1850, when the Swedish opera singer, Jenny Lind, sponsored by P. T. Barnum, the circus magnate, made a triumphant tour of America. Lind was a devout Christian who promoted the music of Lina Sandell and Oscar Ahnfelt, singing their songs at her concerts and other gatherings.

What is Lina Sandell's enduring legacy? When Martin Luther undertook the translation of the New Testament into German during his exile, he said that he wanted its language to be as a mother talking to her children. I believe that that is the enduring legacy of Lina's hymns, so simple that a child could understand. Her songs are filled with images of birds, mother hens, trees, flowers, skies, and stars, and as mentioned before, even God as both mother and father. Her music also speaks to the heart with themes such as God's faithful mercies in times of testing and sorrow, intimate relation to Jesus as brother, friend, and bridegroom, and life as a pilgrimage to the homeland. Her themes were always based on Bible references, sound theology, and Christian experience.

Gracia Grindal, who has translated one of Lina's later hymns still popular in Sweden, spoke of Lina's pure joy in the mercies of God. This song is titled, *"Jag kan icke räkna dem alla"* ("I cannot count them all"). Lina saw a drawing of a little boy saying this while he did sums, and she applied it to the mercies of God. This hymn was the favorite of the more recent translations at all three songfests.

The numberless gifts of God's mercies,
My tongue cannot fathom nor tell.
Like dew that appears in the morning
They come to us shining and full.

Like all of the stars in the heavens,
God's mercies can never be told.
They shine through the darkness of midnight
Their beauties can never grow old.

I'll never count all of God's mercies,
But, O, I can give God my praise!
For all of that love, my thanksgiving
And love to the end of my days.

My hope is that we might find ways in our churches and children's choirs, services of worship and small groups, to keep this legacy alive as we sing her songs, both familiar and less than familiar.

The Numberless Gifts of God's Mercies

WORDS: Lina Sandell, 1832-1903; tr. Gracia Grindal, 1943-, © 1993 Selah Publishing Co., Inc. 9.8.9.8.9.8
MUSIC: Albert Lindström, 1853-1955 Jag Kan Icke Räkna Dem Alla

Gathering at the River

Early in the 1960s I was listening to a classical music station and was stopped dead in my tracks by the deep, mellow voice of the baritone William Warfield singing "Shall We Gather at the River." I later discovered that this was one of four early American songs arranged by Aaron Copland, three of which were sacred, "Simple Gifts," "Zion's Walls," and "At the River." I was surprised that the classical music world had found an old chestnut that we religious folks had by-and-large buried. Though it was in the Covenant Hymnals of 1931 and 1950, it was voted down in the hymnal of 1973. The story behind the hymn is worth telling. Robert Lowry (1826-1899), a Baptist minister, was reflecting on the apocalyptic vision of Revelation 22:1-2: "Then the angel showed me the river of the water of life, bright as crystal, flowing from the throne of God and of the Lamb through the middle of the street of the city."

Carlton R. Young in the *Companion to the United Methodist Hymnal* fills in the details from earlier historical sources:

> On a very hot summer day in 1864, a pastor was seated in his parlor in Brooklyn, New York. It was a time when an epidemic was sweeping through the city, and draping many persons and dwellings in mourning. All around friends and acquaintances were passing away to the spirit land in large numbers. The question began to arise in the heart, with unusual emphasis, "Shall we meet again? We are parting at the river of death, shall we meet at the river of life?"
>
> "Seating myself at the organ," says he, "simply to give vent to the pent of emotions of the heart, the words and music of the hymn began to flow out, as if by inspiration."

Carlton Young points out that most hymnals omit the stanza: "At the smiling of the river, Mirror of the Saviour's face, Saints, whom death will never sever, Lift their songs of saving grace."

I often listen to William Warfield's recording of "At the River." When I discovered that this early American hymn by Robert Lowry had made it across the Atlantic to Sweden, my curiosity was aroused. Hymn writer and composer Joel Blomqvist (1840-1930) was drawn by the text and melody to create a paraphrase of the hymn. In the early 1970s, I bought an LP entitled *Sorgen och Glädjen* ("Sorrow and Gladness") by a Swedish jazz group that played the melody of "At the River" under the title of Blomqvist's *"O hur saligt att få vandra"* ("O How Blest to Be a Pilgrim"). I learned further that his version was in *Sions Basun* and was loved and often sung by our forebears.

I later discovered that my friend Signe Bennett from Chicago's North Park Covenant Church had done some preliminary work translating Blomqvist's paraphrase. It was quite literal and lacked poetry and I felt a strong urge to finish what she had begun. This translation first appeared in *New Hymns and Translations* (1978), then in *The Song Goes On,* and is currently in *The Covenant Hymnal: A Worshipbook* (1996). "O How Blest to Be a Pilgrim" was sung by more than a thousand people in the midnight Service of Holy Communion at the Covenant Centennial in Minneapolis on June 22, 1985.

What commends the Blomqvist paraphrase of "Shall We Gather at the River" is that it fills out the apocalyptic vision of Revelation 22 and removes a certain ambiguity in the original by giving "endless praises to Jesus, who redeemed us by his blood." If the Covenant hymnal commission were convened now, given Signe Bennett's and my own fondness for the Blomqvist paraphrase, I would propose retaining the original "Shall We Gather at the River," placing it side-by-side with "O How Blest to Be a Pilgrim."

Shall We Gather at the River

WORDS: Robert Lowry, 1826-1899
MUSIC: Robert Lowry, 1826-1899

8.7.8.7 with Refrain
Beautiful River

O How Blest to Be a Pilgrim

WORDS: Joel Blomqvist, 1840-1930, Lars P. Ollén, tr. Signe L. Bennett, 1900-1996
Glen V. Wiberg, 1925-, © 1978, 1996 Covenant Publications
MUSIC: Robert Lowry, 1826-1899; arr. Kenneth L. Fenton, 1938-, © 1996 Kenneth Fenton

8.7.8.7 with Refrain
Hanson Place

The Song of Life

On February 26, 2007, several hundred guests attended an extraordinary concert at Landmark Center in St. Paul, Minnesota. The concert with the inviting title, "Listen to the Song of Life," celebrated the life of Bruce Carlson, whose death occurred on July 28, 2006, after a three-year battle with disease. Bruce's thirty-plus years of leadership had put The Schubert Club on the map. He'd brought some of the finest talent in the musical world to the Twin Cities. In addition, he developed The Schubert Club Rare Instruments Museum and took delight in supervising the collection of musical instruments and manuscripts as the museum expanded through the years.

St. Paul's mayor, Chris Coleman, declared the day "Bruce Carlson Day." The pre-concert music consisted of harp, classical guitar, and a trumpet fanfare. The concert program featured a broad and imposing array of Twin Cities musicians, composers, and poets. Several musical sightings moved me greatly. The internationally famous mezzo-soprano Frederica von Stade sang a lovely *lied* by Gustav Mahler and Pulitzer Prize-winning composer Dominick Argento gave a tribute, "Finding the Right Word for Bruce." That right word continued in a "Hymn for Bruce" by composer Stephen Paulus, who accompanied soprano Maria Jette. A soloist at Plymouth Congregational Church in Minneapolis, she appears frequently on Garrison Keillor's radio program, *A Prairie Home Companion.* The text was adapted from the poem "An Offering" by George Herbert (1593-1633). This perfect match of music with text, sung by Maria Jette, brought tears to my eyes. This is the text she sang:

> Since my sadness
> Into gladness
> Lord, thou dost convert,
> O accept
> What thou hast kept,
> As thy due desert.
>
> Had I many,
> Had I any,
> (For this heart is none),
> All would be thine
> And none would be mine:
> Surely thine alone.

Yet thy favor
May give savor
To this poor oblation;
And it raise
To be thy praise,
And be my salvation.

The Schubert Club Notes available at the concert referred to Bruce as "a man of quiet faith." The story that follows gives witness to that faith. Late in the summer, shortly after having been given the disheartening news from his doctors of his worsening condition, Bruce called his staff together around the big wooden table that had been the scene of coffee cups and notebooks for planning future Schubert events. This is how one staff member tells it, "This time was different. Bruce brought to the table an old leather Bible given him by a much-loved Schubert Club Board Member—an early mentor and long-departed friend. Bruce calmly told us his news, and then he read Psalm 100. 'Make a joyful noise unto the Lord, all ye lands…' Next he read the poem 'I Praise' by Rilke. Finally, he read 'The Prayer of Saint Francis.'"

The closing words in Pastor David Hawkinson's homily at Bruce's memorial service at the Plymouth Congregational Church could have also summarized the extraordinary concert celebrating his life "This marvelous, gifted, gracious life, clad in bow-tie and child-like gleam, whose life brought us again and again to say—as we say tonight with tears in our eyes with everything that breathes—Hallelujah!"

Let All the World in Ev'ry Corner Sing

WORDS: George Herbert, 1593-1633
MUSIC: Paul Liljestrand, 1931-2011,

14.12.12.14
Conrad

Rejoice in God's Saints

WORDS: Fred Pratt Green, 1903-2000, © 1973, 1980 Hope Publishing Company
MUSIC: Attributed to William Croft, 1678-1727

10.10.11.11
Hanover

The Song Goes On

Since serving on two hymnal commissions of the Covenant, I've been interested in the publication of new hymnals by a wide spectrum of other church bodies. It's a healthy reminder that the pool for new hymnals is broad and deep and often quite diverse.

In 2006, the Evangelical Lutheran Church in America published a new hymnal. The previous hymnal, the *Lutheran Book of Worship* (the "green" hymnal), was published in 1978. It has been in use 38 years, exceeding the average life of denominational hymnals by 18 years. Work on the 1978 hymnal had begun with the cooperation of The Lutheran Church, Missouri Synod, but it dropped out of the process before publication.

The most common criticism of the *Lutheran Book of Worship* by many Lutherans of Scandinavian background has been the loss of their musical tradition. The scant few hymns in the hymnal leave a trail of hurt feelings behind. I recently received a list of the hymns to be included in this new worship book—*Evangelical Lutheran Worship*. Ardy Johnson, a Covenanter from Carlshend, Michigan, sent me the list. As a fine musician himself, he has accompanied the liturgy and hymns for the Saturday evening service of a nearby Lutheran congregation and has also found a ministry playing in retirement homes. The pastor, knowing Ardy's fervent interest in hymns, gave him the hymn list of the new hymnal. He studied the list and in turn sent it to me.

Of the 655 hymns in the new hymnal, 248—a surprisingly large number—also appear in the Covenant Hymnal. I was surprised to discover 13 gospel songs that have been standard fare among Covenanters for many years on the list. They are as follows:

- Blessed Assurance
- My Hope is built on Nothing Less
- When Peace, like a River
- I Love to Tell the Story
- Shall We Gather at the River
- Rock of Ages, Cleft for Me

- Softly and Tenderly Jesus is Calling
- Amazing Grace
- What a Friend We have in Jesus
- Come, We That Love the Lord (Marching to Zion)
- How Great Thou Art
- Jesus, Savior, Pilot Me
- What a Fellowship, What a Joy Divine

The hymns regarded here as "heritage hymns"—that is, translations from either Swedish, Norwegian or Danish—are sparse in the hymn list. That leaves me wondering how the Augustana hymn tradition, as well as those of the former Norwegian and Danish synods could be by-passed again by their heir, the Evangelical Lutheran Church in America. Only the most familiar hymns are included, such as "Children of the Heavenly Father," "Behold the Host Arrayed in White," "Day by Day," "Thy Holy Wings," "In Heaven Above," "Rejoice, Rejoice, Believers," and "Prepare the Royal Highway" ("Prepare the Way O Zion").

I had hoped to find the Carl Olof Rosenius hymn, "With God as Our Friend," included in the Lutheran "green" hymnal, but missing in the new listing. Also missing is the traditional Christmas Chorale, "All Hail to Thee, O Blessed Morn." No doubt this is due to the disappearance of *Julotta* (the traditional Scandinavian early morning Christmas morning service) from all but a few former Augustana Lutheran churches.

By contrast, readers may be surprised that *The Covenant Hymnal: A Worshipbook* (1996) contains 40 "heritage songs" (due in large part to J. Irving Erickson).

One of the sad omissions in our present hymnal, however, is one of the finest hymns by Lina Sandell. This will appear in the new Lutheran hymnal, translated by my friend and fellow Pietist, Gracia Grindal of Luther Seminary, as "The Numberless Gifts of God's Mercies" *(Jag kan icke räkna dem alla)*. I included the text of this hymn and the story behind it previously and rejoice that it has a place in their new hymnal. After a recent conversation with Gracia, I was left wondering why her voice was not present and heard in the hymnal commission's planning of *Evangelical Lutheran Worship*. She has invited me into a conversation regarding Covenant heritage songs as she prepares for a hymnal to be named Reclaim. The name suggests the effort to recover more of the Lutheran hymnody overlooked by previous hymnal commissions. It will include hymns for the Lectionary. I wish her success in this undertaking.

Finally, I need to celebrate the inclusion in *Evangelical Lutheran Worship* of a new hymn by Jeannette Lindholm, a former member of Salem Covenant Church, New Brighton. In the present *Covenant Hymnal* we have two of her hymns: "We Search for Language to Explain" (445) and "Lord, You Have Welcomed Us" (474) The new hymn, "Unexpected and Mysterious," was premiered with the college orchestra last year at the Christmas concert of Gustavus Adolphus College in St. Peter, Minnesota. It is a lovely Advent hymn.

Hymnals come and go but as long as we have breath, LET THE PEOPLE SING!

Unexpected and Mysterious

WORDS: Jeanette M. Lindholm, 1961-, © Jeanette M. Lindholm, admin. Augsburg Fortress
MUSIC: Calvin Hampton, 1938-1984, © GIA Publications, Inc.

8.7.8.7.D
St. Helena

Surrounded by Angels

I recently observed the use of a new hymn in three services held at the Bethlehem Covenant Church of Minneapolis: a Sunday morning worship service, a funeral, and the blessing of a marriage. I was present at these services and felt in each the awe and wonder of a birthing as a congregation found its song: "Surrounded by God's Silent, Faithful Angels" by Dietrich Bonhoeffer, with music by Siegfried Fietz. Serving as "midwife" for the new hymn was its translator, Pastor Steven Paul Swanson, a member of Bethlehem Covenant Church.

To my knowledge, this is only the second Bonhoeffer hymn that has been translated into English. The first, "By Gracious Powers," has appeared in several recent hymnals: *The United Methodist Hymnal; With One Voice: Supplement of the Lutheran Hymnal; Worship: A Hymnal and Service Book for Roman Catholics; The New Century Hymnal;* and *The Mennonite Hymnal.* We hope this second hymn translated by Swanson will also gain wide usage.

Steve informed me that while serving as pastor of a Free Evangelical congregation in Germany, he found the hymn in a popular hymnal used by many Free Evangelical Churches in Germany—*Ich Will Dir Danken* (Haenssler-Verlag, 1991). He said it is a particular favorite in the Free Churches at New Year's services because of its reference to celebrating the New Year. Steve further stated that Bonhoeffer wrote the poem to his beloved community from prison as a witness to his strong faith and hope of glory, just three months before his martyrdom in 1945.

Asked about his translation, Steve said, "I was literally inspired to translate this hymn when Pastor Phil Stenberg visited me over New Year's in 2000 shortly after the death of his wife, Evonne. As I freely translated the hymn we had sung at our New Year's service, he asked for a written copy. That set me to work and in a night of inspiration at my bedside, the words poured forth. Phil brought the hymn back to the USA that winter..."

These were my three sightings for the hymn. It was sung for the first time by the congregation at the Sunday morning service with the late Dr. F. Burton Nelson of North Park Seminary as preacher, a renowned Bonhoeffer scholar. The second sighting was sung by the Bethlehem choir at the funeral of Carol Swanson, Steve's mother and wife of Paul Swanson, Bible teacher at Minnehaha Academy for many years. The third sighting was at the Celebration and Blessing of the Marriage of Barbara Jean Boca and Steven Paul Swanson when the hymn was again sung. This followed their wedding service at North Park Seminary in Chicago. Steve said, "It also seemed so appropriate to sing it at our wedding, with my mother and both of Barb's parents in the company of heavenly saints, and our wedding date falling on the weekend of All Saints. I love the firm faith which is expressed and confident hope."

A few days following the Celebration and Blessing of Marriage, Barbara and Steve left for Belgium where they would serve the International Church in Belgium.

Recalling the death of our son, Carl, Steve spoke a moving pastoral word to me, concluding with the line from the hymn. "May God continue to bless the memory of our loved one in this season of yearning. May we always remember, 'the world we cannot see breaks through life's boundaries and all God's children sing the glorious song!'"

By Gracious Powers

WORDS: based on Ephesians 5:20, Dietrich Bonhoeffer, 1945, The Cost of Discipleship, 2nd ed., 1959; tr. Fred Pratt Green, 1903-2000,
MUSIC: Charles H. Parry

"May God continue to bless the memory
of our loved one in this season of yearning.
May we always remember, 'the world we cannot
see breaks through life's boundaries and all
God's children sing the glorious song!'"

Surrounded by God's Silent, Faithful Angels

WORDS: Dietrich Bonhoeffer 1906-1945, tr. Steven Swanson
MUSIC: Siegfried Fietz, 1945-

Practice in Christianity

Through my friendship with a good friend, the late Phyllis Holmer, I began a correspondence with a long-standing friend of the Holmers, Dr. Andrew Burgess, Professor of Philosophy and a Kierkegaard scholar at the University of New Mexico in Albuquerque. Dr. Burgess is also a graduate of Minnehaha and was a student of Paul Holmer at the University of Minnesota.

Dr. Burgess' inspiring and insightful essays on the Danish existentialist Søren Kierkegaard (1813-1855) opened up a new territory of treasures to be explored. In my library, I have a significant shelf of Kierkegaard's works, but I have never read anything regarding Moravian influence on him. Burgess' research into this theme relates to the Pietism of the Covenant Church and has prompted me to look more closely at the Moravian influence in our own movement in eighteenth-century Sweden.

In *A History of Christianity,* Kenneth Scott Latourette describes this Pietism as a movement that stressed free grace through the blood of Christ, personal conversion, lay preaching, and conventicle meetings outside the established church. The term "readers" became the designation for its adherents because of the use of the Bible and other Christian literature available at the time. The movement from which our forebears came in 19th century Sweden appears to have been a replay of the century before. The Rosenian revival people were also called "readers," with the similar traits of Pietism demonstrated by the Moravians. But despite the fact that the Moravians in Sweden and Denmark have dwindled, their influence has continued in our hymnody.

In Dr. Burgess' first essay, he demonstrates the amazing development of the role of music in Kierkegaard's early life and later in his writing of *Practice in Christianity.* I had never heard of the Moravian practice of hymn sings or "a song service"*(Syngetime)*, which the Kierkegaard family faithfully attended on Sunday evenings following the Lutheran service in the morning. The description of these song services and how they were conducted with a theme and related verses of hymns was most enticing. With the Moravians, singing hymns with great poetry was apparently more important than preaching. This is explained in the following lovely statement by Dr. Burgess:

> The song services guaranteed that Moravians everywhere would have an extraordinary facility for memorizing and adapting hymns. Kierkegaard's special attraction to Brorson may have come from Kierkegaard's exquisite ear for the sound and rhythm of words, as well as from his appreciation for the ideas expressed. Brorson is a poet of stature, and great poetry stays with a listener one's whole life long.

The trio of Danish composers that Dr. Burgess has discussed in his work—Hans Adolph Brorson (1694-1764), Thomas Kingo (1634-1703), and N.F.S. Grundtvig (1783-1872)—have appeared in our Covenant hymnals as well. Brorson's hymn with the Edvard Grieg setting, "Behold a Host Arrayed in White" is often sung at funerals and on All Saints' Day. Likewise, Kingo's hymns have appeared both in previous hymnals—"Dearest Jesus, Draw Thou Near Me"—and "All who Believe and are Baptized" in our present hymnal. Grundtvig's "Built on the Rock the Church Doth Stand" has appeared in our last three hymnals and is often sung both by the choir and congregation. I was amused by Kierkegaard's preference for hymns by Brorson above those of Grundtvig, speaking of the latter "as jaunty yodeler or a bellowing blacksmith."

The way one observes Kierkegaard's preference for hymns by Brorson above those of Grundtvig with such nuance and hiddenness in the seven expositions of *Practice in Christianity* as well as Dr. Burgess' commentary on the content of the expositions, sent me back to a more careful reading of these lovely discourses. Burgess' moving words uncovered for me an underlying layer to Kierkegaard's writing:

The music from the Danish awakening movements, and particularly Brorson's hymns, is playing in the background of *Practice in Christianity.* To listen is to hear songs of martyrs marching—strangely, a joyful sound. Kierkegaard, too, was attuned to that sound. Records of many other aspects of Kierkegaard's life are lost forever, but we do know the kind of hymns he liked to sing.

In the undergrowth that has grown up around Kierkegaard's writings and in some sad sense of his neglect today, Dr. Burgess has cut a large swath, opening up a pathway to new and fresh discoveries. For this I offer my heartfelt thanks.

Behold a Host Arrayed in White

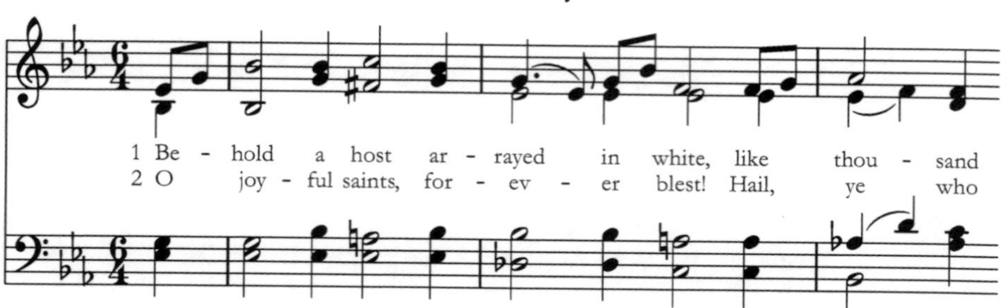

WORDS: Based on Revelation 7:9, Hans Adolf Brorson, 1694-1764,
tr. Carl Doving, 1867-1937, alt.
MUSIC: Norwegian melody, arr. Edvard Grieg, 1843-1907

8.8.8.6.12.L
Behold a Host

The Legacy Lives On

Sweden is an anomaly in many ways, especially as seen and experienced by many American visitors. The most common perception that many Swedish-Americans carry away with them from visiting relatives or friends in the land of their forebears is that today Sweden has become a thoroughly secular place. This is based on how few attend church—except for baptisms, confirmations, weddings, and funerals. As one expression puts it, the job of the church is simply to "hatch, match, and dispatch." While Sweden is often regarded by academics as a model of extreme secularization, it still does things that would strike American observers as alarmingly theocratic. Despite the fact that church and state were formally separated in 2000, Sweden's list of public holidays includes Epiphany, Easter, Ascension, Whitsun/Pentecost, All Saints and Christmas. Though voluntary, Sweden still levies a church tax, collected by the public revenue service. Some 70 percent of citizens still pays this levy, which in effect constitutes membership in a church that is a symbol of national identity.

Having visited a Church of Sweden service on a summer day, the American, whether with sadness, or an anti-Lutheran bias, or an unholy glee reports back home that only five or six attended *högmässa* (high mass). I find it interesting that the "five or six" faithful seem to be the reported number of attendees—no matter what parish in the Church of Sweden one might visit. The "five or six" are the ones universally there! You certainly wouldn't expect any more! So, the conclusion is that when a secular welfare state which meets the needs of all its citizens, whatever one's status, there's an implied question: "Who needs God?"

This point of view would be a hard sell during Advent when churches are often full, where the music of the church fills the air, and where the texts of Advent and the Christmas story seem to be what my historian cousin, Charles Wiberg, describes as being:

> ...a genuine part of the warp and woof of life (with no worries about separating church and state.) As a deeply rooted part of the historic culture of the place, it is not so much a matter of conscious thought or creedal statement, as simply part of life itself. In our own more individualist culture we tend to forget that at the heart of Christmas—and of the whole Biblical epic—it's not so much we who embrace God, as if, like everything else, it were our doing. It is God who has embraced us, from the earliest pages of the Old Testament until this day, a fact that, if comprehended at all, can only be with a sense of awe, wonder, and mystery. Somehow in their bones the Swedes have a sense of that.

These reflections come out of 18 days on an Advent tour led by Eloise and LeRoy Nelson, together with 58 friends, many of whom we knew from previous tours, others from long-standing friendships, and several new friends. Whether in cathedrals or churches, Covenant or Lutheran, or in public places such as the magnificent Blue Hall of the City Hall of Stockholm, or in that city's immense sports hall called *The Globe,* we heard magnificent choral music with small and large choirs with robust Swedish voices of both young and old, singing "Hosianna, David's Son" and even an Advent hymn beloved by Covenanters, "O Zion, Acclaim Your Redeemer," and many other Advent and Christmas hymns and anthems.

We will long remember the soloist Anders Andersson singing "Comfort Ye" from *The Messiah* and *"O Helga Natt"* (O Holy Night) at Immanuel Church in Stockholm; or the glorious concert by a popular jazz saxophonist playing the songs of Advent in the Cathedral in Vaxjö; or attending a rehearsal as the University Choir of Örebro sang the Hallelujah Chorus in traditional and contemporary renditions; or the three choirs with orchestral accompaniment at the City Hall; or the singing of the children along with the unforgettable boy Joseph in the Rättvik Lutheran Church as they enacted the Christmas story (with standing room only); or the amazingly executed concert in The Globe by 1,200 music school students depicting the Light from Haydn's *Creation* to the birth of Jesus, climaxed by John Rutter's thrilling *Gloria.* And these were only the highlights among other moving musical events.

Shortly before the Advent tour, we received a letter from a long-time friend, Jean Barton from Cobalt, Connecticut, describing a concert by a well-known rock band that she and her daughter attended in Stockholm in December. The concert was not Jean's choice but a celebration with her daughter who had just completed an exchange program at the Mission Covenant's college in Jönköping, *Södra Vätterbygdens Folkhögskola.* Their seats were in the front row of the concert hall, where Jean reports the sound was deafening. At the intermission, a small portable organ was brought center stage and a band member sat down and began singing *"Härlig är Jorden"* (a Swedish hymn to the tune of "Beautiful Savior") to which the whole young audience joined in singing one of Sweden's most loved hymns. Needless to say, there were tears in the eyes of both Jean and her daughter.

So the most skeptical might ask of this anomaly, "Where does this outpouring of psalms, hymns, and spiritual songs come from?" After three such Advent tours, the only answer I can come up with is this: it must come from something in the yearning soul of Sweden, something like the parable Jesus told of the treasure hidden in the field which lends value to the whole field. It comes from remembering the buried treasure, a legacy that is still alive.

O Zion, Acclaim Your Redeemer!

1 O Zi - on, ac - claim your Re - deem - er! Je -
2 He comes from the joys of the a - ges, he
3 He comes as a ran - som most ho - ly, he
4 He comes from the tomb as a vic - tor, the
5 He comes to the sor - row - ing spir - it and
ru - sa - lem, wel - come your King! Strew palms on the way for the
leaves his do - min - ion sub - lime; from glo - ry to Beth - le - hem's
dies on the cross for the world; re - demp - tion from sin is ac -
shad - ows of death clear a - way; the slum - ber - ing saints are a -
life is re-newed by his hand; he comes to es - tab - lish a
Sav - ior, his prais - es ex - ul - tant - ly sing,
man - ger he comes in the full - ness of time.
com - plished, his ban - ner of light is un - furled.
wak - ened, a - roused from their sleep in the clay.
King - dom that shall thro' e - ter - ni - ty stand.
Refrain
Re - joice! Re - joice! Re - joice in your Sav - ior and King! Re -

WORDS: Mary Elizabeth Servoss, 1849-1906, tr. Erik Nyström, 1842-1907,
E. Gustav Johnson, 1893-1974, © 1950, 1996 Covenant Publications
MUSIC: James McGranahan, 1840-1907; arr. Norman E. Johnson, 1928-1983,
© 1973, 1996 Covenant Publications

9.8.9.8. with Refrain
Gå Sion

Prepare the Way, O Zion!

WORDS: Frans Mikael Franzén, 1772-1847, tr. Augustus Nelson, 1863-1949
MUSIC: Swedish melody, 1694 from *Svenskapsalmboken,* 1697;
arr. *American Lutheran Hymnal,* 1930

7.6.7.6.7.7.6.6
Bereden Väg För Herran

"Thinking globally invites new singing locally. We have a new and wonderful opportunity to renew and energize our worship by connecting with brothers and sisters in Christ from around the world, as we pause in our giving and become receivers from these fellow Christians."

Thinking Globally, Singing Locally

In May 2002, Royce Eckhardt, then Minister of Music at the Winnetka Presbyterian Church, and I conducted a "50s-plus" conference at Pilgrim Pines on ethnic music in *The Covenant Hymnal: A Worshipbook*. The theme we chose was "Thinking Globally and Singing Locally." Thinking globally has been, and still is, central to our Christian proclamation and mission. However, with the entry into our vocabulary of the concept of globalization, it has new relevance, particularly as the term "global village" seems suddenly real and near—right at our doorstep.

New faces from different parts of the world are appearing in our congregations in Minneapolis and Saint Paul. They represent groups from different parts of the world: Sudanese, Laotians, Hmong, Somalis, and others. Faced with a new opportunity for ministry, pastors and lay people are asking: How can we offer hospitality in welcoming these new immigrants into our community of faith? There is a growing sense among many Christians that God is doing something new. We find ourselves tested and also enriched by hearing new voices and by experiencing other traditions of the larger global church.

Thinking globally invites new singing locally. We have a new and wonderful opportunity to renew and energize our worship by connecting with brothers and sisters in Christ from around the world, as we pause in our giving and become receivers from these fellow Christians.

Furthermore, as receivers, we have the opportunity to welcome music from our own neighborhood as well as from other parts of the world as a gift of the Holy Spirit. New sounds, new rhythms, new texts, and new movements invite us to recognize the Body of Christ as one with many parts. Mindful that our worship experiences, whether traditional or contemporary, can become narrow and provincial, Royce and I proceeded in the hope that, during our three-day workshop among seniors, we might open some new doors and windows in congregational singing. We proceeded in faith that the new hymnal could become an instrument for stretching, a musical workout for flabby spiritual muscles.

We had both served on the hymnal commission, so we were well acquainted with our intentions in preparing a hymnal and worship book for the 21st century, namely, setting the table for African-Americans, Hispanics, West Indians, Ghanaians, South Africans, Koreans, among others, as well as providing for our tradition's musical needs.

What happens when we learn to sing the songs of other ethnic groups? I believe it serves the Gospel in overcoming racism. If we sing songs of other ethnic groups in Sunday worship, it will shape how we see and work beside these persons of different backgrounds. In other words, by music we build bridges that enable us to meet—not as strangers or outsiders, but more than neighbors—as sisters and brothers in Christ.

Royce and I confessed fears that by using some 26 ethnic songs that were new to the seniors, some of them challenging, given their diversity of styles, we might encounter some resistance, perhaps anger. Our fears were groundless. It was wonderful to hear these seniors lift their voices in a Hispanic/Brazilian hymn, "We Worship Only You," written by Jorge Maldonado, a gifted musician, ecumenist, and a Covenanter. It was also moving to hear them sing a Russian *Kyrie* ("Lord, have mercy") in a responsive reading of Psalm 109.

I was especially touched by the singing of another Hispanic hymn, "You Have Come." It is a hymn that brings us to the lake shore of Galilee, where we hear the call of Jesus to the disciples to leave possessions behind—boats, nets, labor, gold, and weapons—in order to follow him. In the refrain, there is one of the most remarkable phrases, one I have never heard before in any hymns or sermons—an image of a smiling Christ.

> O Lord, with your eyes you have searched me,
> And while smiling have spoken my name;
> Now my boat's left on the shoreline behind me;
> By your side I will seek other seas.

The Scandinavian heritage has a great musical tradition as well, evidenced much already in this book. We explored that hymnody at this event, introducing "Gathered in God's Presence," written by two Norwegians, Sveim Ellingsen and Egil Hovland, who composed the hymn in 1993 for the Winter Olympics held in Lillehammer, Norway. They use the strong metaphor of "torch of promise" in the refrain in verse 4: "bear the flame now kindled as light to all the nations."

We were overwhelmed by the response to the workshop. The East Coast seniors demonstrated flexibility, zest, and eagerness to learn new things.

Seguirte Solo a Tí (We Worship Only You)

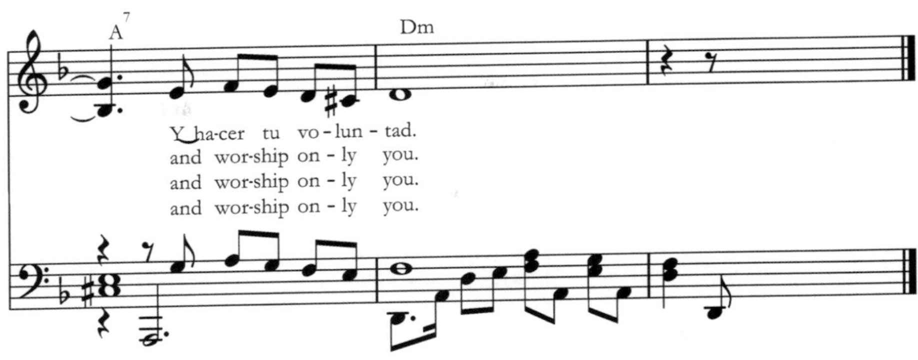

NOTE: Roland Tabell, the arranger, informed *Pietisten* of an error in this song as it appears in *The Covenant Hymnal* (1996). The chord in the second measure should be an A7, and the bass note in that same measure should be an A. We've corrected these mistakes for the version printed in this volume.

Communicating the Story

The research of Philip J. Anderson, professor of Church History at North Park Seminary in Chicago, has focused on how the Pietistic renewal and revival heritage from the 1840s and the experience of immigration has given a rich texture of meaning to the metaphors of God, Christ, and the pilgrimage of faith. They have formed a key component in the hymnody of the Covenant Church from the beginning. Inviting discussion about our church's singing today, Phil asks, "What is communicated in the story of faith?"

This question should embrace all musical genres, if we wish to avoid the artificial and often alienating bifurcations of old and new, traditional and contemporary. We should consider how and why decisions are made by those who select music and plan worship, as well as analyze in a critical, constructive way. What is the substantive content of the story of faith? In these decisions, matters of Christian identity are at stake, and some set of criteria therefore becomes crucial to what is collectively sung in our gatherings.

Referring to Saint Paul's words in I Corinthians 13 that faith, hope, and love abide, he offers a critique in all that is sung and done, namely, "What must I believe?" "What must I hope?" "What must I do?"

A similar theme can be seen in "An Open Letter to Covenant Church Leaders Regarding Our Hymnody," by Covenant pastor and church planter Andrew Thompson of Wenatchee, Washington. His letter was written in response to Phil Anderson's question regarding the Covenant's musical history. The letter expresses the hope that we heed Anderson's reminders and pro-actively consider how we might deepen and enrich this important aspect of our weekly worship, theological reflection, and catechism. In the worship life of many of our churches, singing has taken on almost as central a place as preaching. For many parishioners, the lyrics of the songs we sing are committed to memory as much or more than scripture. We know that our songs are important. They shape how we engage faith. They shape our doctrinal focus and our devotional lives. They shape our praxis. They shape us. But it seems that as a denomination, we are doing little to shape our songs.

Thompson's letter continues on to refer to worship in a contemporary setting that has been shaped by a wide usage of music from Mercy/Vineyard publishing and Hillsong music. The songs of these communities are catchy, singable, widely distributed. As such they are shaping our churches to be remade in the image of the Vineyard and Hillsong communities, and potentially distancing us from our homegrown theology.

Thompson's letter included a challenge to build up our tradition of hymnody of Covenant song by supporting homegrown contemporary hymnwriters, among them, Bryan Leech, Jim Black, Richard Carlson, Bob Stromberg, Dennis Moon. This could be done by introducing indigenous music at Covenant events. Thompson suggested inviting submissions of songs from Covenant congregations prior to its national conferences such as Midwinter, the Annual Meeting, and the Feast. The criteria for evaluating these songs would be 1) singability 2) theological content and integrity to Covenant heritage 3) relevance to the themes of the meetings. One or two top selected songs could be highlighted in worship and made available to participants by CDs or sheet music.

He offered a further suggestion to help pastors grow by offering a "theology of song writing" course at North Park Seminary or as part of the orientation program for pastors coming into the Covenant.

Continuing on in this theme, let us consider a well-known Covenant musician and highly esteemed member of two hymnal commissions, Royce Eckhardt. With input from musicians, historians, theologians and pastors, he has been studying the songs of Covenanters asking, "Where is the Covenant heading in the area of worship music and liturgical matters?" He proposes to create and implement a denomination-wide teaching emphasis on Christian worship: workshops and seminars, articles for the denominational magazine (Covenant Companion), primary emphasis at nationwide conferences, and special courses for North Park Theological Seminary. While strongly supporting Thompson's call to create opportunities and venues for the encouragement and usage of our own Covenant's hymnic gifts, Eckhardt also calls us "to be aware of the rich treasury given us by the larger church, even the global church, lest in our denominational gatherings and local churches we become parochial and ignore the great contemporary hymnody that already exists."

Finally, I must bear witness (and I think many would agree) to the truth that, grounded in the Biblical story, Covenant hymnody has shaped our theology, given us comfort and hope in times of testing and grief, and inspired and empowered our mission. I hope by reclaiming the hymnal as an educational tool as well as a worship book, we will expose our young people and new believers to this rich and diverse legacy lest it be lost. As Phil Anderson has said so forcefully, "In these decisions, matters of Christian identity are at stake."

Come, Celebrate the Presence of the Lord

In unison
1 Come, cel - e - brate the pres - ence of the Lord whose Ho - ly Spir - it draws us all to - geth - er. One faith, one Lord, our hope has been re - stored as gifts of love up - on us have been poured. Come,
2 Come, cel - e - brate the good - ness of the Lord whose strong and lov - ing arms are put a - round us. Held in God's care who hears our ev - 'ry prayer and lifts us up to glo - ry from de - spair. Come,
3 Come, cel - e - brate the mer - cy of the Lord whose ev - er - last - ing cov - e - nant is giv - en. Sin quar - an - tined but God has in - ter - vened, in Je - sus' name we now have been re - deemed. Come,
4 Come, cel - e - brate the glo - ry of the Lord whose king - dom is be - yond our un - der - stand - ing. Wit - ness the show'r of bless - ing and of pow'r, for God is pres - ent with us in this hour. Come,

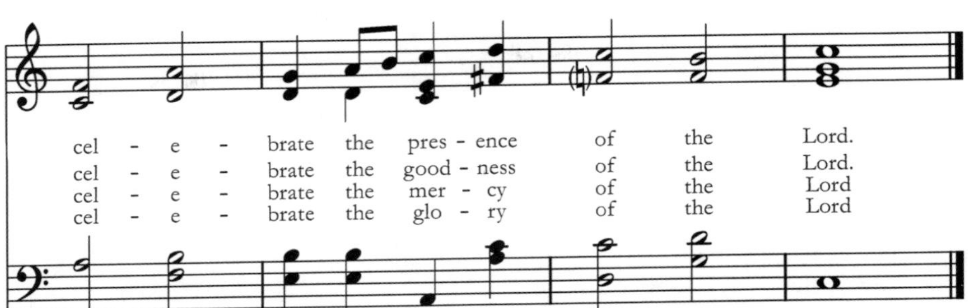
cel - e - brate the pres - ence of the Lord.
cel - e - brate the good - ness of the Lord.
cel - e - brate the mer - cy of the Lord
cel - e - brate the glo - ry of the Lord

10.11.10.10.10
Over Texas

Welcome Sinners

As a lover of hymns, I've learned to tread gently in offering critiques of hymns, especially those in popular usage. Gracia Grindal, Professor of Rhetoric at Luther Seminary, St. Paul, has recently raised a question in *The Christian Century* about the hymn, "Amazing Grace," one that has won such universal approval, even by people who do not consider themselves Christians. One hears it at state funerals and other solemn national occasions as an affirmation of general grace, leading Grindal to ask the question, "Whose grace?"

The composer of the hymn, John Newton, most certainly intended it to be a witness to the saving grace of Jesus Christ. Grindal would not discourage its public usage, but wonders if those hearing the hymn might ask whose grace is being referred to and in searching, discover Jesus. But she thinks that might be a stretch. Yet, for those within the believing community who have been found by such amazing grace, the hymn remains a robust and joyous witness.

This witness of the hymn has recently been playing in the secular world of advertising. In the welter of commercials for teeth whitening, tooth paste, insurance, attorneys, soaps, and fast foods, one becomes aware of the hymn playing in the background of our imaginations. "Amazing Grace," not sung, but spoken, by several witnesses who once were lost, but now are found, blind, but now they see. What made the witness so real was taking each word of the hymn and personalizing it by their own experience, with their own sense of lost-ness and failure, but now found and rescued. One could have expected an appeal for funds or a plug for an institution, but the surprise at the end was simply the words "The Salvation Army." Through the power of the hymn "Amazing Grace" there was only good news: "Welcome Sinners." I have no doubt that John Newton would have approved.

One of the most remarkable books I've read in recent years is N.T. Wright's *Surprised by Hope: Rethinking Heaven, the Resurrection, the Mission of the Church.* To my surprise, this Anglican bishop critiques several popular hymns, including "How Great Thou Art," made popular by the Billy Graham Crusades and George Beverly Shea. Shea sang the best-known translation by Stuart K. Hines. I think that this song runs a second to "Amazing Grace" in its popularity and usage in ceremonial occasions such as funerals, both in church and in non-church settings.

N.T. Wright sounds this warning:

> Some of the hymns in the revivalist and charismatic traditions slip into the easy mistake, cognate as we shall see with misleading view of the "second coming," of suggesting that Jesus will return to take his people away from earth and "home" to heaven. Thus that wonderful hymn, "How Great Thou Art," in its final stanza declares:
>
> When Christ shall come, with shout of acclamation,
> And take me home, what joy shall fill my heart.
> (Wright, *Surprised by Hope,* p. 22.)

As mentioned earlier, the original was written by an early Covenant pastor in Sweden, a gifted writer, composer of hymns, and preacher, Carl Boberg (1859-1940). Speaking of this final verse of the hymn, Wright makes the point in keeping with the original Swedish: the song doesn't talk about Christ coming to take me home, but speaks rather of "the veils of time falling, faith being changed into clear sight, and the bells of eternity summoning us to our Sabbath rest." Wright says it has a lot more to recommend it (see literal translation). And then he offers his own second line to Boberg's final verse:

> When Christ shall come, with shout of acclamation,
> And heal this world, what joy will fill my heart.

This anticipates Wright's later argument that Christ's coming again has a larger purpose than taking us out of this world. Rather, the purpose is to bring to fulfillment the New Creation of New Heavens and a New Earth. This is also Carl Boberg's vision in verse 7 of the original.

> When I behold thy Son to earth descending
> To heal and save and teach distressed mankind,
> When evil fleas and death is seen recoiling
> Before the glory of the Lord divine.

The promise of "Amazing Grace" is not fulfilled by the added verse of John Newton's, "When we've been there ten thousand years, bright shining as the sun, we've no less days to sing God's praise than when we first begun." (John P. Rees 1859-?) Rather, the promise is of the New Creation, New Heavens, and a New Earth. Meanwhile: Welcome, sinners! We have a grand future and a great continuing task!

Amazing Grace! How Sweet the Sound

WORDS: John Newton, 1725-1807, st. 5, John P. Rees, 1780
MUSIC: American melody, 1831; arr. Edwin O. Excell, 1851-1921

C.M.
Amazing Grace

Epilogue: A Rich Legacy

When I asked Carleton R. Young, editor of the 1989 Methodist hymnal, whether the use of overheads in worship might not make singing from hymnals obsolete, he said, "We have all the technology to do so, but when the light of the overhead goes off, I have nothing in my hands. However, when I take up my hymnal in song and prayer, I hold 2,000 years of church history in my hands."

The following list of authors, composers, and translators might seem wasted time and effort. But to some, it celebrates the rich legacy of history and communion of saints—anticipating and continuing well beyond the millennia—raising heavenly songs of high praise to God and the Lamb. This treasure is worth caring about and passing on to coming generations.

Moving from the second to the third millennium in the Christian era provided me an occasion to take note of hymnic anniversaries with a focus on years ending with "25," "50," "75," and "00." With the help of a Lutheran Cantor and hymnologist, Mark Filbert, I offer a partial list of anniversaries from our own Covenant Hymnal. The dates are followed by a number in parentheses indicating the anniversary as of the year 2000.

375 (1625th): Synesius of Cyrene was born. He was the author of "Lord Jesus, Think on Me."

700 (1300th): The Venerable Bede may have written "A Hymn of Glory Let Us Sing."

750 (1250th): Theodulph of Orleans, probable author of "All Glory Laud and Honor," was born.

1150 (850th): Bernard of Clairvaux may have written the poem from which three hymns have been drawn, including "Jesus, O Joy of Loving Hearts."

1225 (775th): Francis of Assisi wrote "All Creatures of Our God and King."

1550 (450th): Nikolaus Decius was born. He authored "All Glory Be to God on High" and "O Lamb of God, Most Holy."

1625 (375th): Johan Rudolph Ahle, who wrote "Blessed Jesus, at Your Word," was born.

1650 (350th): Joachim Neander, author of "Praise to the Lord, the Almighty" and "Open Now Your Gates of Beauty," was born.

1700 (300th): Nicolaus Ludwig von Zinzendorf, patron and bishop of the Moravian Church and author of "Jesus, Your Blood and Righteousness," was born. Timothy Dwight was born. He wrote "I Love Your Kingdom, Lord." John Newton was born, author of "Amazing Grace," "One There Is Above All Others," "How Sweet the Name of Jesus Sounds," "Glorious Things of You Are Spoken," and "May the Grace of Christ, Our Savior."

1750 (250th): Johann Sebastian Bach died. He composed and arranged existing tunes, such as "O Morning Star, How Fair and Bright," "O Sacred Head, Now Wounded," and several others.

1800 (200th): John Goss was born. He was a musical editor of hymns and author of "Praise My Soul, the King of Heaven," (melody also used for "Thanks to God Whose Word Was Spoken" and "May God's Love Be Fixed Above You") and "See, Amid the Winter Snow." Matthew Bridges, who authored the original version of "Crown Him with Many Crowns," was born. William Billings, who composed "When Jesus Wept," died. William Cowper, author of "God Moves in a Mysterious Way" and "Sometimes a Light Surprises," died. Dimitri S. Borniansky, composer of the Vesper Hymn whose melody is used with a hymn by Bryan Jeffery Leech, "We Are Part of God's Creation," died.

1850 (150th): Andeliga Sånger (Spiritual Songs) was published by Oscar Ahnfelt and underwritten by another famous Swede, the operatic singer Jenny Lind. The volume contained 12 songs with piano or guitar accompaniment and included Ahnfelt's tune, "With God as Our Friend." Bessie Porter Head was born. She wrote "O Breath of Life." Frank Mason North, author of "Where Cross the Crowded Ways of Life," was born. Daniel Brink Towner was born. He authored "Trust and Obey."

1875 (125th): Philip P. Bliss wrote "Man of Sorrows, 'What a Name'" and its accompanying tune, "Hallelujah! What a Savior!" Martin Edward Shaw was born. He was a hymnal editor who prepared numerous harmonizations that continue in common use, such as "All Things Bright and Beautiful," and "God is Working His Purpose Out." John Samuel Monsell died. He authored many hymns including "Sing to the Lord of Harvest" and "On Our Way Rejoicing." Joseph P. Webster, author of "There's a Land That Is Fairer Than Day," died.

1900 (100th): James Weldon Johnson wrote "Lift Every Voice and Sing," which has become a particularly cherished anthem for African-Americans. David Elton

Trueblood, author of "God, Whose Purpose is to Kindle," was born. Samuel John Stone, author of "The Church's One Foundation," died. Henry Twells, author of "At Evening When the Sun Was Set," died.

1925 (75th): The Hymnal and Order of Service was published by the Augustana Lutheran Church in Rock Island, Illinois. Of significance to Covenanters is the fact that of the 663 hymns, 73 were English translations of Swedish originals. Among the translations were "Holy Majesty, Before You" and "Children of the Heavenly Father." Thomas Stevenson Colvin was born. He compiled four collections of African hymns and composed "Jesu, Jesu, Fill Us with Your Love." Alice Parker was born. She arranged hundreds of hymns, often with Robert Shaw, including "My Lord of Light" and "Forgive Our Sins as We Forgive." Zenos Hawkinson, who translated "Now Comes the Time for Flowers," was born. A certain Glen Wiberg was even born this year, translator of "Jesus of Nazareth Passes By," "How Great the Joy," "O How Blest To Be a Pilgrim," and others. Samuel Trevor Francis died. He wrote "O the Deep, Deep Love of Jesus." John Wesley Work, Jr. died, the arranger of "When Israel Was in Egypt's Land" and "Go Tell It on the Mountain."

1950 (50th): Marty Haugen was born. He wrote many contemporary hymns such as "Halle-, Halle-, Hallelujah," "You Are the Salt of the Earth, O People," "Healer of Our Every Ill," "Gather Us In," and others. Hugh Thomson Kerr, author of "God of Our Life, through All the Circling Years," died. Graham Kendrick, author of "Shine, Jesus, Shine," was born. With hymnals in hand and songs—assembled from a long, rich history— in our hearts, we are ready for the new millennium.

Fill the Earth with Music

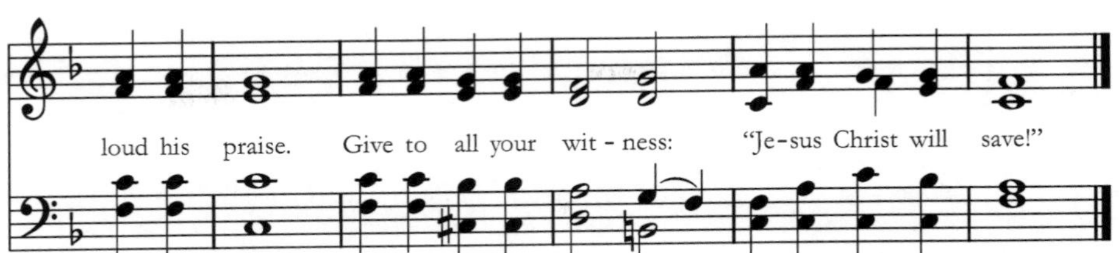

WORDS: R. G. Huff, 1949-,
MUSIC: James Mountain, 1844-1933

6.5.6.5.D. with Refrain
Wye Valley

Let the Whole Creation Cry

WORDS: Stopford A. Brooke, 1832-1916, alt.
MUSIC: Jakob Hintze, 1622-1702; arr. Johann Sebastian Bach, 1685-1750

7.7.7.7.D
Salzburg

Appendix: Recommended Recordings

Here is a sampling of excellent CD recordings of much of the music discussed in this book and more, compiled by the staff of *Pietisten*.

(These recordings may be difficult to find in North America, but can often be found by visiting the websites or stores of Scandinavian distributors and booksellers, including Verbum, Gummessons, Wessmans, Gehrmans, Gospel Center, as well as Naxos and other distributors listed below. "Sounds of Sweden" and "Best of Julfest" are available by contacting Pietisten *directly.)*

Andeliga Sånger av Lina Sandell och Oscar Ahnfelt. Proprius 1996.
(A classic radio broadcast from the 1960s of the Gothenburg Chamber Choir with Soprano Ingegerd Tyrenius and Baritone Bo Ohlgren, performing 23 of the "Spiritual Songs" of Ahnfelt and Sandell. Swedish.)

Best of Julfest: Music of a Scandinavian Christmas. First Covenant Church, Seattle 2006.
(A compilation of live recordings from the annual Julfest Advent Service at First Covenant Church of Seattle, Washington. Contact Pietisten*. Swedish and English.)*

Blott en dag. Carola. Universal Music 2001.
(Swedish pop musician Carola's contemporary rendition of 12 Lina Sandell songs, masterfully delivered with pipe organ and electric guitar accompaniment. Swedish.)

Bred dina vida vingar: Göteborgs Gosskör sjunger Psalmer och Andliga sånger. Naxos 2000.
(17 "Spiritual Songs" of Ahnfelt and Sandell, as well as several other universally beloved hymns, are performed by the Gothenburg Cathedral Boys Choir and Baritone Olle Persson. Swedish.)

Dagen är kommen: Göteborgs Domkyrkas Gosskör sjunger julsånger. Naxos 1996.
(The Gothenburg Cathedral Boys Choir and Baritone Olle Persson deliver 20 classic Christmas songs. Swedish and English.)

Det går en sång över världen: O Store Gud. Zamba Studio 1999.
(A collection of songs by Carl Boberg, featuring several versions of his best known hymn, "How Great Thou Art," which has been translated into at least 100 languages. Swedish, English, German, Filipino and Albanian.)

Folkjul: A Swedish Folk Christmas. BIS Northern Lights 2007.
(A forward-looking interpretation of 15 traditional Christmas tunes, mixing both contemporary styles and ancient Scandinavian folk music settings. Swedish and Latin.)

Jul, Jul… Anders Andersson, Mats Nilssons Vokalensemble. Verbum, Signatur, Linx Music 1995.
(Soloist Anders Andersson and the Mats Nilsson Vocal Ensemble deliver this essential collection of 19 Christmas songs, recorded in the iconic Immanuel Church in Stockholm. Swedish.)

Nearer, Still Nearer: Hymns, Songs and Liturgy from the Augustana Heritage Association 2004 Gathering at Gustavus Adolphus College, St. Peter, Minnesota. Augustana Heritage Association 2006.
(A collection of Scandinavian and North American hymn classics recorded live, including some of the translated Swedish Lutheran liturgy, widely used by the Augustana Lutheran Church. English.)

Norrsken: SVF Musiklinjens Kör. Södra Vätterbygdens Folkhögskola 2007.
(A stunning collection of 21 traditional and contemporary Christmas classics, performed by the talented choir of Southern Vättern College of Jönköping, Sweden. This CD contains much of the music performed on their 2007 and 2008 Advent concert tours of the United States. Swedish and English.)

Ovan där: Minnesalbum. Artur Erikson. Soloist, Verbum.
(This tribute collection features 24 songs of the Swedish Awakening and American gospel classics, performed by Soloist Artur Erikson and choir in the 1970s. Swedish.)

Sounds of Sweden: Featuring Oscar Ahnfelt and His Spiritual Songs. *Pietisten* 1994.
(18 sacred and secular songs recorded in concert at First Covenant Church of St. Paul, Minnesota, performed by Soprano Christina Ekström and Guitarist Bo Haraldsson—as they were meant to be played! Swedish and English.)

Swedish Folk Tunes from Dalecarlia. Proprius, Gehrmans 2004.
(The Uppsala Cathedral Choir and Organist Andrew Canning perform several hymns set to traditional folk tunes, arranged by Nils Lindberg. Swedish.)

Ur Davids Psalmer. A Selection from the Psalms of David by Gunnar Wennerberg. Proprius 1995.
(The Malmö Chamber Choir and Soloists Göran Stenlund, Bo Ohlgren and Anders Eriksson perform these classic anthems by one of the Swedish Awakening's most celebrated choral composers, Gunnar Wennerberg. Swedish.)

Årets Krans: Danske Salmer. Københavns Drengekor. Danica Records 1997.
(21 hymns by N.F.S. Grundtvig and Hans Adolph Brorson, among others, by the Boys Choir of Copenhagen, directed by Ebbe Munk. Danish.)

Älskade psalmer från tonhallen, Sundsvall. Verbum, Naxos 1995.
(A great choir of 450 voices, directed by Kjell Lönnå, accompanied by the Järfälla Gospel Brass, perform 11 beloved hymns. Swedish.)

Copyright Owners and Administrators

A.B. Nordiska Musikforlaget, represented by Gehrmans Musikförlag AB
www.gehrmans.se
Jesus of Nazareth Passes By (music)

Augsburg Fortress
www.augsburgfortress.org
Children of the Heavenly Father (translation)
Thy Holy Wings, Dear Savior (translation)
Unexpected and Mysterious (text)
Wheresoe'er I Roam (translation)
With God as Our Friend (translation)

Concordia Publishing House
www.cph.org
Lord of All Gladness (music)
At the Lamb's High Feast (arrangement)

Covenant Publications
www.covchurch.org/publications/
How Great the Joy (translation)
I Sing With Joy and Gladness (translation)
Jesus of Nazareth Passes By (translation)
O How Blest to Be a Pilgrim (translation)
O Let Your Soul Now Be Filled with Gladness (arrangement, translation)
O Mighty God, When I Behold the Wonder (translation)
O Zion, Acclaim Your Redeemer (arrangement, translation)
With God as Our Friend (arrangement)

GIA Publications, Inc.
www.giamusic.com
Unexpected and Mysterious (music)

Hark! Productions
150 62nd Ave. NE
St. Petersburg, FL 33702
Come Celebrate the Presence of the Lord

Hope Publishing Company
www.hopepublishing.com
By Gracious Powers (translation)
How Great Thou Art
Let All the World (music)
Rejoice in God's Saints (text)

LifeWay Christian Resources
www.lifeway.com
Fill the Earth With Music (text)

Jorge Maldonado
jorgeynoris@yahoo.com
We Worship Only You (text)

Kenneth Fenton
3100 85th Ave N #227
Brooklyn Park, MN 55443
O How Blest to Be a Pilgrim (arrangement)

Roland Tabell
RolandArts@aol.com
We Worship Only You (arrangement)

Selah Publishing Co.
www.selahpub.com
The Numberless Gifts of God's Mercies (translation)

Singspiration Music/ASCAP, represented by Music Services
www.musicservices.org
He the Pearly Gates Will Open (arrangement)

William K. Provine
Thy Holy Wings, Dear Savior (arrangement)

About the Author

An ordained pastor since 1953, Rev. Glen V. Wiberg has served Covenant churches in Haddam Neck, Connecticut, Princeton, Illinois, Youngstown, Ohio, Chicago, Illinois (North Park), and New Brighton, Minnesota. Rev. Wiberg served on three hymnal commissions (for the 1973 and 1996 hymnals, as well as the 1990 *The Song Goes On* supplement) for the Evangelical Covenant Church. He has translated a number of hymns from Swedish, and four of his translations appear in the most recent *Covenant Hymnal.* He is also the author of *Called to Be His People* (1970), *This Side of the River: a Centennial Story, Salem Covenant Church, 1888-1988* (1995), and *Housing the Sacred: What I Have Learned and Still Am Learning About Preaching* (2009). Rev. Wiberg lives in New Brighton with his wife Jane.

About Pietisten

Pietisten, Inc. is a 501(c)(3) non-profit and the publisher of the twice-yearly journal of the same name.

Pietisten is ecumenical and does not formally represent any institution, but it draws heavy inspiration from the collective heritage of Lutheran Pietism, as represented in a congenial flock of historically-related traditions: the Evangelical Covenant Church and Svenska Missionskyrkan (Mission Covenant Church of Sweden), the Augustana Lutheran heritage (ELCA), the Evangelical Free Church, and the Baptist General Conference, and epidemics of Pietism within the Congregationalist and Methodist folds. *Pietisten* is the spiritual heir of a Swedish devotional newspaper of the same name, published between 1842-1918.

www.pietisten.org

Acknowledgments

Publisher: Karl Nelson

Copyeditor: John Markuson

Layout and Cover Design: Sandy Nelson

Editorial Assistance: Steph Blomgren, Chris Brown, Bonnie Nelson, David Nelson, Eric Nelson, Mark Safstrom

Music Engraving: Phil Holmes, Karl Nelson, Kieren MacMillan, Mike O'Donnel, Michael Roy

Patrons:

Dorothy Balch

Robert Dvorak

Matt and Kathie Frank

James and Sandra Holst

Phil and Sandy Johnson

G. Timothy Johnson

Gordon and Chris Johnson

Elder and Muriel Lindahl

Bryce and Bonnie Nelson

Kristine Pugh

Index

A

A History of Christianity 106
Ahle, Johan Rudolph 127
Ahnfelt, Oscar 13, 14, 15, 17, 22, 25, 51, 86, 128, 133, 134
A Hymn of Glory Let Us Sing 127
Alas! And Did My Savior Bleed 75
All Creatures of Our God and King 127
All Glory Be to God on High 127
All Glory Laud and Honor 127
All Hail to Thee, O Blessed Morn 97
All Things Bright and Beautiful 128
All who Believe and are Baptized 107
Amazing Grace! How Sweet the Sound 97, 124, 125, 126, 128
And Can It Be That I Should Gain 72
Anderson, Carl Philip 30
Anderson, Philip J. 8, 30, 120, 121
Andersson, Anders 111, 134
A Prairie Home Companion 92
Are You Washed in the Blood 69
Argento, Dominick 92
Aschan, Peter Jonsson 19, 43
At Evening When the Sun Was Set 129
At the Lamb's High Feast 35, 77, 135
At the River 88
Augustana Heritage Association 8, 134
Augustana Lutheran Church 8, 22, 85, 129, 134
Augustine 44

B

Bach, Johann Sebastian 128, 132
Barnum, P. T. 86
Basun, Sions 4, 18, 85, 89
Beautiful Savior 111
Behold a Host Arrayed in White 107, 108
Behold the Host Arrayed in White 97
Bennett, Signe L. 79, 89, 91
Bernard of Clairvaux 127
Bethlehem Covenant Church 58, 100
Bethlehem Mission Covenant Church 26
Billings, William 128
Black, Jim 121
Blessed Assurance 96, 97
Blessed Jesus, at Your Word 127
Bliss, Philip P. 128
Blom, Fredrik A. 84
Blomqvist, Joel 89
Boberg, Carl 59, 61, 63, 64, 65, 125, 133
Bohemian Brethren's Kirchensänge 77
Bonhoeffer, Dietrich 100, 102, 105
Borniansky, Dimitri S. 128
Brödraförsamlingen 71
Brooke, Stopford A. 132
Brorson, Adolph 107, 134
Brorson, Hans Adolf 109
Buber, Martin 9
Built on the Rock the Church Doth Stand 107
Burgess, Andrew 106, 107
By Gracious Powers 100, 102, 136

C

Caedmon's Hymn 57, 58
Calvin, John 45
Campbell, Robert 77
Campbell, Thomas 73
Carlson, Bruce 1, 92
Carlson, Nathaniel 84
Carlson, Richard K. 121, 123
Carola 22, 133
Central Lutheran Church 85
Children of the Heavenly Father 3, 22, 48, 50, 51, 52, 54, 85, 97, 129, 135
Chosen Seed and Zion's Children 20
Church of Sweden 14, 18, 44, 63, 78, 85, 110, 137
Colvin, Thomas Stevenson 129
Come, Celebrate the Presence of the Lord 122
Come, We That Love the Lord (Marching to Zion) 97
Come, You Faithful, Raise the Strain 34, 35
Comfort Ye 111
Companion to the United Methodist Hymnal 88
Copland, Aaron 88
Covenant Church 1, 2, 4, 8, 9, 19, 26, 40, 41, 44, 58, 63, 69, 82, 83, 85, 89, 98, 100, 106, 120, 133, 134, 137

Covenant Hymnal 2, 9, 15, 22, 27, 30, 34, 35, 52, 59, 63, 64, 65, 69, 75, 88, 89, 96, 97, 98, 116, 119, 127, 137
Cowper, William 74, 128
Croft, William 95
Crown Him with Many Crowns 128

D

Dannström, Johan Isidor 7
Davies, James P. 13
Day by Day and with Each Passing Moment 22, 23, 24, 48, 51, 85, 97
Dearest Jesus, Draw Thou Near Me 107
Decius, Nikolaus 127
Dickey, Mark S. 28
Doving, Carl 109
Dwight, Timothy 128

E

Ecclesiastical History of the English People 59
Eckhardt, Royce 40, 43, 116, 117, 121
Ellingsen, Sveim 117
Enquist, Per Olof 18
Erickson, Artur 44
Erickson, J. Irving 1, 2, 4, 9, 19, 40, 41, 85, 97
Erling, Bernhard 8
Evangelical Covenant Church 1, 2, 8, 40, 137
Evangelical Free Church 82, 85, 137
Evangelical Lutheran Church in America 96, 97
Evangelical Lutheran Worship 34, 35, 96, 97, 98
Evangeliska Fosterlands-Stiftelsen 18, 85

F

Fenton, Kenneth L. 91
Fietz, Siegfried 100, 105
Fill the Earth with Music 130, 136
First Covenant Church, Minneapolis 40
First Covenant Church of Kansas City 4, 82
First Evangelical Free Church of Minneapolis 82
Forgive Our Sins as We Forgive 129
Fortunatus 75, 76
Foss, Claude W. 20
Francis of Assisi 127
Francis, Samuel Trevor 129
Franzén, Frans Mikael 114
Frostenson, Anders 9, 78, 80
Frykman, Andrew T. 62
Frykman, Nils 44, 45, 47, 62, 78, 79, 81

G

Gastoldi, Giovanni G. 31, 33
Gathered in God's Presence 117
Gather Us In 129
Gerhardt, Paul 74
Gesangbuch 37
Glorious Things of You Are Spoken 128
God is Working His Purpose Out 128
God Moves in a Mysterious Way 128
God of Our Life, through All the Circling Years 129
God, Whose Purpose is to Kindle 129
Goss, John 128
Go Tell It on the Mountain 129
Graham, Billy 63, 124
Great Hills May Tremble 48
Green, Fred Pratt 95, 102
Grieg, Edvard 107, 109
Grindal, Gracia 27, 51, 85, 86, 87, 97, 124
Grundtvig, N.F.S. 107, 134
Gustavus Adolphus College 8, 98, 134

H

Halle-, Halle-, Hallelujah 129
Hallelujah! What a Savior 128
Hampton, Calvin 99
Härlig är Jorden 111
Haugen, Marty 129
Hawkinson, David 93
Hawkinson, Eric 44, 45
Hawkinson, Zenos 129
Healer of Our Every Ill 129
Hemlandssånger 85
Herbert, George 92, 94
He the Pearly Gates Will Open 82, 84, 136
Hines, Stuart 64
Hintze, Jakob 132
Holmer, Paul 106
Holy Majesty, Before You 129
Hosianna, David's Son 111
Hovland, Egil 117
How Great the Joy 44, 46, 129, 135
How Great Thou Art 51, 58, 60, 63, 64, 97, 124, 125, 133, 136
How Sweet the Name of Jesus Sounds 128
Huff, R. G. 131

I

Ich Will Dir Danken 100
If Asked Whereon I Rest My Claim 70, 71
I Love to Tell the Story 96
I Love Your Kingdom, Lord 128
Immanuel Church 44, 45, 78, 111, 134
In Heaven Above 97
In Thee is Gladness 30
In the Lord's Courts 4
See also What Joy There Is

I Sing with Joy and Gladness 78, 81, 135
I Surrender All 41

J

Jesu, Jesu, Fill Us with Your Love 129
Jesus of Nazareth Passes By 9, 78, 80, 129, 135
Jesus, O Joy of Loving Hearts 127
Jesus Priceless Treasure 79
Jesus, Savior, Pilot Me 97
Jesus, Your Blood and Righteousness 128
Jette, Maria 92
John of Damascus 37, 38
Johnson, E. Gustav 59, 63, 64, 65, 78, 79, 81, 113
Johnson, James Weldon 128
Johnson, Norman 84

K

Keillor, Garrison 92
Kendrick, Graham 129
Kerr, Hugh Thomson 129
Kierkegaard, Søren 106, 107
Kingo, Thomas 107

L

Larson, Winifred 82, 83
Larsson, Carl 26
Latourette, Kenneth Scott 106
Leech, Bryan Jeffery 121, 128
Let All the World in Ev'ry Corner Sing 94, 136
Let the Whole Creation Cry 132
Lewi's Journey 18, 19
Lift Every Voice and Sing 128
Liljestrand, Paul 94
Lindemann, Johann 30, 33
Lindholm, Jeanette M. 98, 99
Lind, Jenny 86, 128
Lindström, Albert 87
Lofsånger 47
Lord, As a Pilgrim 9, 27
Lord Jesus, Think on Me 127
Lord of All Gladness 30, 32, 135
Lord, You Have Welcomed Us 98
Lowry, Robert 88, 90, 91
Lund University 18
Lutheran Book of Worship 13, 51, 85, 96
Lutheran Church of America 8
Luther, Martin 86
Luther Seminary 27, 51, 85, 97, 124

M

Mahler, Gustav 92
Maldonado, Jorge E. 117, 119, 136
Man of Sorrows, What a Name 128
Markuson, Aaron 44, 45, 47
Marty, Martin 79
May God's Love Be Fixed Above You 128
May the Grace of Christ, Our Savior 128
McGranahan, James 113
Mission Covenant Church of Sweden 44, 63, 85, 137
Mission Hymns 22
Monsell, John Samuel 128
Moody, Dwight L. 2
Moon, Dennis 121
Moravian 14, 18, 19, 22, 40, 69, 70, 75, 106, 107, 128
More Secure Is No One Ever 55
Mountain, James 131
My Crucified Savior 69
My Hope is built on Nothing Less 96
My Lord of Light 129

N

Neale, John M. 37, 38
Neale, John Mason 76
Neander, Joachim 128
Nelson, Augustus 114
Nelson, F. Burton 100
Nelson, Wesley 78
New Hymns and Translations 89
Newton, John 124, 125, 126, 128
Niebuhr, H. Richard 34
Nordqvist, Gustaf L. 80
Norman E. Johnson 113
Norris, Kathleen 74, 75
Northbrook Covenant Church 44
North Park College 40, 78
North Park Covenant Church 79, 82, 83, 89
North Park Seminary 8, 44, 100, 101, 120, 121
North Park Theological Seminary 54, 121
Nothing but the Blood of Jesus 69
Now Comes the Time for Flowers 129
Now Thank We All Our God 79
Nyström, Erik 113

O

O Breath of Life 128
O Come, All Ye Faithful 78
O Holy Night 111
O How Blest to Be a Pilgrim 3, 79, 88, 91, 129, 135, 136
O Lamb of God, Most Holy 127
O Let Your Soul Now Be Filled with Gladness 3, 18, 19, 40, 42, 45, 70, 135
Ollén, Lars P. 91
Olsen-Dulin, Alfred 84
Olson, Ernst W. 50
Olsson, Karl A. 2, 3, 14, 18, 40, 43, 45, 69

O Mighty God 51, 59, 63, 64, 65, 68
O Morning Star, How Fair and Bright 128
One There Is Above All Others 128
On Our Way Rejoicing 128
Open Now Your Gates of Beauty 128
O Sacred Head, Now Wounded 128
O Tender, Gracious Father 22
O the Deep, Deep Love of Jesus 129
Our Mighty God Works Mighty Wonders 62
O Zion, Acclaim Your Redeemer 111, 112, 135

P

Parker, Alice 129
Parry, Charles H. 102
Paulus, Stephen 92
Peace Corps 58
Peterson, Victor O. 17
Plymouth Congregational Church 92, 93
Porter Head, Bessie 128
Power in the Blood 69
Praise My Soul, the King of Heaven 128
Praise to the Lord, the Almighty 79, 128
Prepare the Royal Highway 97
Prepare the Way, O Zion 114

R

Rees, John P. 125, 126
Reformed Church in America 64
Rejoice in God's Saints 95, 136
Rejoice in the Lord 64
Rejoice, Rejoice, Believers 97
Rock of Ages, Cleft for Me 96
Rosenius, Carl Olof 9, 13, 14, 15, 17, 19, 51, 97
Routley, Eric 64
Runeberg, Johan Ludvig 7
Rutström, Anders Carl 20
Ryden, Ernest Edwin 9, 27

S

Safstrom, Mark 1, 53, 67, 138
Salem Covenant Church 85, 98, 137
Sandell, Lina 3, 9, 14, 21, 22, 23, 25, 27, 28, 48, 50, 51, 53, 54, 55, 56, 85, 86, 87, 97, 133
Sånger, Andeliga 22, 128, 133
Scandinavian Augustana Evangelical Lutheran Synod
See also Augustana Lutheran Church
See, Amid the Winter Snow 128
Seguirte Solo a Tí (We Worship Only You) 117, 118, 136
Selander, Inger 18
Servoss, Mary Elizabeth 113
Shall We Gather at the River 88, 89, 90, 96
Shaw, Martin Edward 128
Shaw, Robert 129
Shea, George Beverly 63, 124
Shine, Jesus, Shine 129
Simple Gifts 88
Sing it Again 1
Sing My Tongue 75
Sing My Tongue, the Glorious Battle 76
Sing to the Lord of Harvest 128
Sions Nya Sånger 20
Skoog, A. L. 62
Skoog, A.L. 22, 25
Smart, Henry T. 38
Södra Vätterbygdens Folkhögskola 111, 134
Softly and Tenderly Jesus is Calling 97
Sometimes a Light Surprises 128
Songs of Moses and the Lamb 14, 75
Spiritual Songs 14, 22, 128, 133, 134
Steven Paul Swanson 100
St. Olaf College 26
Stone, Samuel John 129
Stromberg, Bob 121
Stuart K. Hine 61, 63
Surely No One Can Be Safer 51
Surrounded by God's Silent, Faithful Angels 100, 104
Swanson, Steven 100, 105
Swedish Evangelical Mission Covenant Church of America
See also Evangelical Covenant Church
Synesius of Cyrene 127

T

Tabell, Roland 119, 136
Tales of the Hasidim 9
Thanks to God Whose Word Was Spoken 128
The Christian Century 124
The Church's One Foundation 129
The Covenant Hymnal 2, 9, 15, 30, 34, 35, 52, 59, 63, 64, 65, 69, 75, 89, 97, 116, 119
The Covenant Hymnal: A Worshipbook 15, 30, 69, 89, 97, 116
The Day of Resurrection 34, 38
The Evangelical Homeland Foundation 18, 85
The Highest Joy That Can Be Known 79
The Lutheran Church, Missouri Synod 96
The Mennonite Hymnal 100
The New Century Hymnal 51, 52, 54, 63, 64, 68, 100
The Numberless Gifts of God's Mercies 86, 87, 97, 136
Theodulph of Orleans 127
There is a Fountain Filled with Blood 69, 74
There's a Land That Is Fairer Than Day 128
The Song Goes On 1, 30, 45, 89, 96, 137

The Songs of Moses and the Lamb 14
The Story of Christian Hymnody 9, 14
The Swedish Psalmbook 2, 14, 15, 53
The United Methodist Hymnal; With One Voice 100
The Venerable Bede 59, 127
This Far by Faith 69
Thorwall, A. J. 82
Thou Tender, Gracious Father 48
Thy Holy Wings, Dear Savior 9, 22, 27, 28, 48, 51, 85, 97, 135, 136
Towner, Daniel Brink 128
Trueblood, David Elton 128
Trust and Obey 128
Tryggare kan ingen vara 49, 51, 53
Twells, Henry 129
Twice Born Hymns 9

U

Unexpected and Mysterious 98, 99, 135
United Church of Christ 51, 63
University of New Mexico 106
University of Oslo 26

V

Venantius Honorius Fortunatus 76
von Stade, Frederica 92
von Zinzendorf, Nicolaus Ludwig 128

W

Waldenström, Paul Peter 70, 85
Wallgren, A. Samuel 7, 71
Wallin, Johan Olof 9, 14, 15
Warfield, William 88
Watts, Isaac 74, 75
We Are Part of God's Creation 128
Webster, Joseph P. 128
We Search for Language to Explain 98
Wesley, Charles 73
We Worship Only You 117, 136
What a Fellowship, What a Joy Divine 97
What a Friend We have in Jesus 97
What Joy There Is 4, 6
When Israel Was in Egypt's Land 129
When I Survey the Wondrous Cross 74
When Jesus Wept 128
When Peace, like a River 96
Where is the Friend for Whom I'm Ever Yearning 9
Wheresoe'er I Roam 9, 14, 15, 16, 135
Wiberg, Charles 110
Wiberg, Jane 26
Wiberg, Rev. Glen V. 1, 33, 47, 80, 91, 129, 137
Winkworth, Catherine 30, 33, 79
Winnetka Covenant Church 41
Winnetka Presbyterian Church 116
With God as Our Friend 6, 12, 51, 97, 128, 135
With One Voice 51, 85, 100
Work, Jr., John Wesley 129
Worship: A Hymnal and Service Book for Roman Catholics 100
Wright, N.T. 124

Y

Yale Divinity School 34
You Are the Salt of the Earth, O People 129
Young, Carlton R. 88, 127

Z

Zions Nya Sånger 71
Zion's Walls 88
Zwingli 30

Made in the USA
Charleston, SC
25 August 2011